THE NON CON PACK

A BUG OUT BAG FOR WHEN COMING HOME IS NO LONGER AN OPTION

DROPSToNE PRESS
The NonCon Pack: A Bug Out Bag for When Coming Home is No Longer an Option
Creek Stewart

Copy editor: Jacob Perry
Contributing Author: Jesse Alphin
Contributing Author: Stephen Kinney
Layout and Design: River Design Company

Wholesale purchases can be made at www.ingramcontent.com.
Purchase this manual and others in this series at http://www.creekstewart.com.

Published by DROPSToNE PRESS
978-1-947281-11-0

DROPSToNE
— P R E S S —
dropstonepress.com

WARNING:

A NONCON PACK is designed for a life-and-death survival scenario. Some of the skills, tools, ideas, and suggestions in this book should ONLY be used in a real life survival scenario. Be sure to check and abide by all state and federal laws regarding legality of any items or skills featured in this manual.

TABLE OF CONTENTS

TABLE OF CONTENTS

INTROD

UCTION

You've likely heard the phrase "Bug Out Bag." It's a term that describes a survival backpack, filled with supplies, designed to sustain an individual for three days of independent survival in the event of a large-scale disaster. Many of the items stowed in a Bug Out Bag are consumable. For example, one typically packs enough food and water to last for three days, enough fuel for small stoves to cook a limited supply of meals, a stock of disposable first aid supplies, a limited supply of ammunition, and several other consumable items to meet basic needs. For many, once several days of independent survival have passed, most of the Bug Out Bag supplies will have been consumed. If the time line for surviving stretches longer than 72 hours, it's not hard to see how this could be a problem.

I consider the NONCON Pack the "next layer" of survival preparedness, when compared to a Bug Out Bag. It's certainly not for everyone. NONCON stands for NON-CONSUMABLES. Thus, a NONCON backpack is stocked with non-consumable items, the sole purpose of which will be the securing of consumables for long-term survival. In theory, a NONCON Pack is designed to sustain someone indefinitely—or at least a lot longer than a three-day Bug Out Bag. As the author of the best-selling book, **Build the Perfect Bug Out Bag**, I am the world's biggest advocate for keeping a 72-hour survival kit packed and ready to go at a moment's notice. However, a nagging question always remained in the back of my mind: *what if something so terrible, catastrophic, and horrific happened that coming back home was no longer an option?* Is it likely? No. Is it possible? Of course, it is. As someone who strongly believes in the importance of preparedness, this question posed a problem for me.

To answer this tough question, my challenge of carefully testing and selecting an assortment of non-consumable products, supplies, and tools began. These things had to be able to provide for as many of my consumable needs as possible, but they also had to fit into a pack that I could carry on my back for reasonable distances at a time. This manual is the collective result of my experimentation and findings. It is essentially a blueprint for exactly how I've built my personal NONCON Pack and how I plan to use the tools and supplies within it to secure consumables such as food, water, fuel, etc. From here on out in this manual, I've listed and detailed everything that is in my own pack and why it made the cut. Is it perfect? No. Is it a darn good NONCON Pack? Yes.

While building a NONCON Pack may be considered extreme by some, I didn't build my pack for those people. I built it for myself and the people I love. Having spent nearly five years thinking, testing, building, choosing, and tinkering with this project, I'm proud of the result.

I have written this manual for two reasons: 1) I hope that it inspires others to be more prepared for the day when the unexpected happens and that their odds of surviving improve because of it. **2)** I've spent a lot of time and money testing and choosing the products for my NONCON Pack, and I hope that by sharing my observations, it will save others time and money, should they choose to build a similar pack.

For your convenience, I have provided a list of links to many of the products (with the exception of custom, one-of-a-kind or after market items) mentioned throughout this manual on my web-site at: **http://www.creekstewart.com/noncon-list.**

Let's get started!

A NOTE ABOUT FIREARMS

For most people, firearms and ammunition are a part of any survival plan and packing strategy. However, because ammunition is consumable, I have not included a firearms category in this NONCON Manual (but I have included one unique firearm in my pack, which I think you will thoroughly enjoy). Yes, firearms ARE a part of my survival gear, and I'd never leave home to face a potential survival scenario without several of them. However, for this manual, I want to adhere to the rules of NONCON as much as possible. Firearms and ammunition are certainly an exception to the NONCON rules.

CHAPTER 1

THE PACK

One of the biggest challenges I faced during the entire pack-building process was choosing a pack that was large enough to carry what I needed yet comfortable enough to be practical. I've hiked hundreds of miles with over 15 different backpack arrangements for this project, and I have learned a lot about what works and what doesn't work for my personal tastes.

I can't say enough about the importance of pack choice when it comes to rucking the amount of gear required for a NONCON scenario. If you choose the wrong pack, nothing else matters. There are many different backpack brands, styles, and configurations that will work for a NONCON pack. This chapter details the style I have decided to use.

Admittedly, I had almost given up on my search for a pack that I was completely happy with, until a friend, Jesse Alphin, introduced me to the concept of a modified ALICE pack. I have never, in all my life and travels, met someone as knowledgeable about backpacks as Jesse. ALICE stands for All-Purpose Lightweight Individual Carry Equipment, and it was the pack system used by the United States Army from 1973 until the MOLLE system was introduced many years later. I have used an ALICE Pack once, when I was a Boy Scout, and I must say that it was the most uncomfortable thing I've ever strapped on my body. It hurt my neck, back, shoulders, and every other body part with which it came into contact. The buckles were very difficult to use, so I ultimately decided to leave the pockets unbuckled because of the hassle. For over 20 years, until an enlightening conversation with Jesse, I've equated the ALICE pack system with misery and discomfort.

Maybe it was because I had tried to block the ALICE Pack from my memory altogether, but unbeknownst to me, the ALICE system has made a comeback on the surplus market. However, a variety of modifications now make this pack one of the most functional, comfortable, and versatile packs I've ever strapped on my back—AND one of the least expensive, too! Many modern packs are ridiculously overpriced!

Unmodified Medium ALICE Pack (left) and Deluxe Build Modified ALICE Pack (right) .

Creek wearing MH (Modified Hybrid) ALICE Basic Build.

There is no avoiding the simple fact that a NONCON pack will be heavy. Thus, the backpack is at the core of the entire build, and starting with the right pack makes everything else—from storing and organizing gear to eventually rucking it over the river and through the woods to grandma's house—easier. I'm sure there are other packs that will do the job, but my favorites have become a variety of modified ALICE systems. They're very fun to build and modify, and almost everything you could want is available through ARMY/NAVY surplus channels or internet auction sites at reasonable prices. Building your own pack is a fun project, and the result is something custom tailored to your tastes.

I asked my friend, Jesse, to put together his own version of a NONCON Pack, specifically for readers of this manual, using parts and pieces available on the surplus market. The amount of knowledge and research packed (pun intended) into the next portion of this manual (written by Jesse) is mind-blowing! He has basically written an instruction manual for the average consumer, detailing how to build one of the most robust and functional backpacks available in the world today. Ladies and Gentlemen, I'd like to introduce to you the MH (Modified Hybrid) ALICE RUCKSAK and instructions, written by Jesse Alphin. This information alone is worth the price of this book.

A few of my favorite packs that didn't make the NONCON cut.

MODIFIED HYBRID ALICE RUCKSACK (MH ALICE)

BY JESSE ALPHIN, TRADEHAWKER.COM

The LC-1/LC-2 US Medium ALICE rucksack makes a fine platform for load-bearing needs. The rucksack is just the fabric portion of the pack. The frame should be removed and replaced with the Enduroflex™ frame. When combined with the modular flexibility of the Enduroflex™ frame, MOLLE II components can then be added for a robust NONCON load-bearing system. The designation MH ALICE (Modified Hybrid ALICE) will be used for the following NONCON system build.

Unmodified ALICE Pack (medium).

Medium ALICE frame with pack removed.

Generally, there are two build options for an **MH ALICE rucksack:** The Basic Build and the Deluxe Build. These two choices are determined by the space (cubic inches) needed (and/or funds available) for the NONCON system. Both are detailed below.

MH ALICE Components:
BASIC BUILD

A) **1-ALICE LC-1/LC-2 Medium Rucksack:** The LC-1/LC-2 Medium ALICE rucksack provides 1,500 cubic inches of space in the main rucksack body, and a total of 2,635 cubic inches of space for load-bearing (main rucksack + 3 outer pockets + lid) in the NONCON system. The Medium ALICE was originally designed for use with or without the LC-1 aluminum pack frame. For the MH ALICE build, only the basic rucksack is needed. The shoulder straps and the waist belt are not utilized. If a complete Medium ALICE rucksack system is available (Medium ALICE rucksack, LC-1 ALICE frame, shoulder straps, and waist belt), remove the Medium ALICE rucksack from the frame and stow the rest for spares or future builds. Check the entire Medium ALICE ruck for tears, holes, broken snaps, weak Velcro™ strips, and torn or cut webbing straps. Here is a good rule to follow: if there are more than 3 areas of damage to a Medium ALICE rucksack, then look for another with less damage (preferably none) to the main rucksack. Most damaged ALICE rucks can be repaired for future use. However, the start of a build is not the opportune time for repairs. Look for the best Medium ALICE ruck for your MH ALICE build and you will not be disappointed.

LC-1 and early LC-2 ALICE rucks are OD green. Sometime around the late 1980s, the LC-1/LC-2 ALICE rucks were changed over to a BDU (Woodland) camouflage. The National/NATO Stocking Number (NSN) for an LC-1 Medium ALICE is 8465-00-001-6480. The NSN for the LC-2 Medium ALICE is 8465-01-019-9102. The NSN for the LC-1/LC-2 Medium ALICE in BDU camouflage is 8465-01-253-5335. The designation of LC-1 or LC-2 in a Medium ALICE rucksack is not a concern for the MH ALICE build. These designations represent minor changes in the overall rucksack system over decades of contracts for the US Department of Defense. Use any of the listed NSN numbers on an internet search engine to find the Medium ALICE rucksack of your choice; both LC-1 and LC-2 Medium ALICE rucksacks will work as a suitable base for an MH ALICE build in the NONCON system.

Enduroflex™ Frame

US MOLLE II Shoulder Straps

MH ALICE Components:
BASIC BUILD *CONTINUED*

B) **1-Ram-Flex™ Frame or Enduroflex™ Frame (Coleman/ Outdoor Products):** The Enduroflex™ frame serves as the backbone of the MH ALICE system. There are few backpacking frames that provide the combination of strength, durability, modularity, low weight, and minimal profile (all at an economical price point) found in the Enduroflex™ frame. Coleman originally marketed this frame as the Ram-Flex™ frame with their Peak 1™ backpack series throughout the 1980s and well into the 1990s. The quality of Peak 1™ packs was underwhelming, but the frames were an engineering marvel. Today, this frame is occasionally marketed with Outdoor Products backpacks. The Enduroflex™ name is used instead of Ram-Flex™ and Outdoor Products also slightly changed the frame design on later backpack models. There are three common Enduroflex™ frame heights found today: 35 inches (this is the oldest Coleman Peak 1™ model), 27 ½ inches (this is the last Coleman Peak 1™ model), and 29 inches (this is the Outdoor Products redesigned Enduroflex™ model). Although all three of the Enduroflex ™ frames mentioned are suitable for an MH ALICE build, the 27 ½ inch frame is the ideal frame for this NONCON system. All Enduroflex™ frames are black in color.

C) **1-US MOLLE II Shoulder Straps (with load-stabilizers):** The US MOLLE II shoulder straps are used in the US Army's (currently issued) MOLLE II load-bearing/existence system. These shoulder straps are well-designed, and provide a solid base for the MH ALICE build. The BDU camouflage US MOLLE II shoulder strap unit is listed as NSN 8465-01-465-2133 and includes a set of BDU MOLLE II shoulder straps and a pair of OD green load stabilizer straps (with D rings). The stabilizer straps are almost always missing from the shoulder straps in the used surplus market. An easy replacement for these hard-to-find straps are the ACU camouflage load lifter attachments listed under NSN 8465-01-524-7241. These (load lifters) easily mount to the top of the MH ALICE frame to utilize the MOLLE II shoulder straps' load stabilizer webbing.

MH ALICE Components:
BASIC BUILD CONTINUED

D) 1-US MOLLE II Waist Belt: The US MOLLE II waist belt is also currently used in the US MOLLE II load-bearing/existence system. This waist belt is well-engineered, featuring a segmented system of padding along the sides and a thick area of padding around the lumbar area. The narrow portion of this belt should be toward the ground when mounted. When bought on the surplus market, there should be an inspection for wear in the lumbar padding, as well as the webbing along the rear of the belt. The waist belt buckle should be replaced with a FASTEX MOLLE II Waist Belt Buckle. The BDU camouflage US MOLLE II waist belt is listed under NSN 8465-01-465-2109.

E) 1-US MOLLE II Sleep System Carrier: The US MOLLE II Sleep System Carrier is currently used to secure the US Army's Modular Sleep System when utilized on the MOLLE II rucksack (for training/deployment). When completely expanded, this sleep carrier supplies over 2,800 cubic inches of space. Its design is like a horizontally mounted duffel bag. This Cordura™ made unit has a rain flap and a cinch tight webbing system to minimize bulk. The US MOLLE II Sleep System Carrier is horizontally loaded and has a water repellent treatment in its interior. Lightweight, bulky items are easily stowed in this system. Since it is currently used to carry the 4 piece US Army Modular Sleep System, it can easily handle any commercial sleeping bag or sleep system with ample room for extra necessities. The BDU US MOLLE II Sleep System Carrier is listed under NSN 8465-01-465-2124.

F) 5-FASTEX MOLLE II Replacement Buckles: These buckles are used in the MH ALICE build as replacements for the old ALICE buckle/webbing system. Currently, these buckles are listed under NSN 8465-01-465-2080 and NSN 8465-01-524-7639. The previous NSN numbers are listings for repair kits in the MOLLE II load-bearing system, which contain: 4 ITW NEXUS FASTEX side release repair buckles, 2 FASTEX Ladderloc™ buckles, and 1 ITW NEXUS FASTEX MOLLE II waist belt buckle. To get 5 ITW NEXUS FASTEX buckles for the ALICE webbing (3 front pockets and 2 main rucksack straps), two replacement kits are needed, since they are only provided in sets of 4. The singular difference between the FASTEX buckles in the previously listed NSNs is usually the color: DCU (desert camo tan) and ACU (grey).

MOLLE Waist Belt

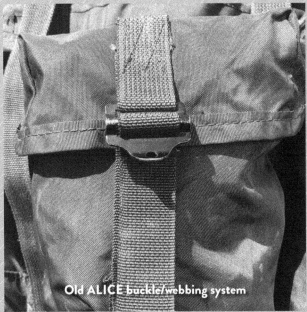

Old ALICE buckle/webbing system

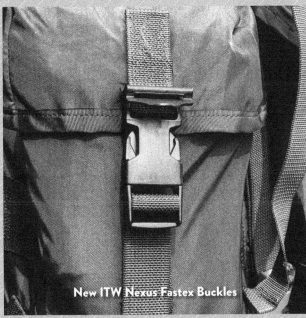

New ITW Nexus Fastex Buckles

Sleep System

MH ALICE Components:
BASIC BUILD *CONTINUED*

G) 1-FASTEX MOLLE II Waist Belt Buckle: The early BDU US MOLLE II waist belts were supplied with Lock Monster™ buckles. These buckles were serviceable but were later replaced with FASTEX ITW NEXUS waist belt buckles. FASTEX ITW NEXUS waist belt buckles are a superior design over the older Lock Monster™ buckle, due to their center press button release instead of the older side press release. The NSN 8465-01-465-2080 and NSN 8465-01-524-7639 MOLLE II buckle repair kits usually contain the FASTEX ITW NEXUS waist belt buckle. This buckle should replace any older MOLLE II waist belt buckles in the MH ALICE build.

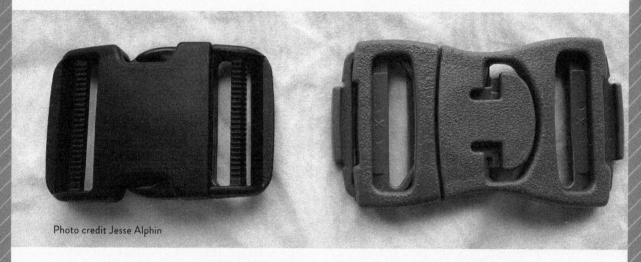

Photo credit Jesse Alphin

Lock Monster™ buckle (LEFT), FASTEX ITW NEXUS waist belt buckle (RIGHT).

MH ALICE Components:
DELUXE BUILD *(SUGGESTED BUT FLEXIBLE)*

MH ALICE Basic Build (left) and MH ALICE Deluxe Build (right).

MH ALICE Components:
DELUXE BUILD *(SUGGESTED BUT FLEXIBLE)* CONTINUED

COMPONENTS OF THE BASIC BUILD (as listed in previous section)

A) **1-ALICE LC-1/LC-2 Medium Rucksack**

B) **1-Enduroflex™ (Coleman/ Outdoor Products)**

C) **1-US MOLLE II Shoulder Straps (with load stabilizers)**

D) **1-US MOLLE II Waist Belt**

E) **1-US MOLLE II Sleep Carrier System**

F) **5-FASTEX MOLLE II Replacement Buckles**

G) **1-FASTEX MOLLE II Waist Belt Buckle**

(The Following are Additional Components for the Deluxe Build)

H) **1-US Field Training Pack/ALICE and IIFS compatible:** The US Field Training Pack was fielded as a component of the IIFS load-bearing system during the late 1980s and early 1990s. The IIFS system was supposed to replace all ALICE gear, but both systems were utilized until the MOLLE system was commissioned. All IIFS gear is compatible with ALICE webbing. The US Field Training Pack provides 672 cubic inches of space with a drawstring rain cover, a water-resistant interior, and a lid with dual FASTEX buckle closures. This pack is easily attached to the Medium ALICE rucksack lid using the existing webbing. The US Field Training Pack is listed under NSN 8465-00-935-6825.

MH ALICE Components:
DELUXE BUILD *(SUGGESTED BUT FLEXIBLE)* CONTINUED

I) **1-US MOLLE II Medical Pouch:** This medical pouch is currently issued in the US MOLLE II system. There are at least 2 sizes found in the surplus market. The larger of the two is listed under NSN 6532-01-467-4988. The larger pouch provides 137 cubic inches of space and has a Velcro™ attachment with a Velcro™ top (for First-Aid designation/EMT/Trauma patches). The US MOLLE II Medical Pouch easily attaches to the left or right top of the Medium ALICE rucksack webbing.

J) **1-US MOLLE II SAW Pouch -or- 1 US General Purpose Large Pouch:** These pouches provide roughly the same number of cubic inches (137) as the large US MOLLE II Medical Pouch. On the surplus market, the SAW pouch is easier to find. They are listed under NSN 8465-01-459-6580 (SAW Pouch) and NSN 8465-01-F01-0320 (GP Large). Either of these pouches can be attached to the left or right top of the Medium ALICE rucksack webbing.

K) **1-Spec-Ops Brand H.U.M.P. Hydration Carrier:** This hydration unit carrier is a commercial unit made of 1000 denier Cordura™ manufactured by Spec-OPS® Brand. The name H.U.M.P. is an acronym for Hydration Utility Multiple Platform. The H.U.M.P. system is ALICE and MOLLE II compatible, and can carry both US Military and Commercial hydration units up to 3 liters in volume or provide 183 cubic inches of cargo space. The H.U.M.P. unit is mounted in the center (square) portion of the Enduroflex™ frame underneath the US MOLLE II shoulder straps.

US MOLLE II SAW Pouch

US MOLLE II Medical Pouch

US MOLLE II Waistpack

US ALICE waterproof bag liner used as emergency cache to store goods for later in hollow stump.

MH ALICE Components:
OPTIONAL *(SUGGESTED BUT FLEXIBLE)*

A) US MOLLE II Sustainment Pouches (2 or more): These Cordura™ pouches provide 900 cubic inches of space in the US MOLLE II load-bearing system. The US Military uses these pouches for carrying Meal(s) Ready to Eat, or MRE(s). Sustainment pouches have a paracord drawstring top closure, a water repellent interior, and a FASTEX buckle attachment lid. There are multiple uses for these pouches. They are used in the MH ALICE build as stuff sacks in the main ruck for future use in the field. The (BDU camouflage) US MOLLE II Sustainment Pouch is listed under NSN 8465-01-465-2152.

B) US MOLLE II Waist Pack (1 or more): The US MOLLE II Waist Pack (or Butt Pack) is made of Cordura™ and provides 468 cubic inches of space in the US MOLLE II load-bearing system. The obvious use for this unit is waist (front) or lumbar (rear) carry. In the MH ALICE build, this unit attaches to the upper Medium ALICE rucksack webbing, under the lid (a second can be stowed in the main rucksack for future use or carried around the waist). This waist belt system is well designed, incorporating a horizontal YKK™ zipper closure underneath 2 horizontal FASTEX buckle attachments. The belt is left and right side adjustable, with a Lock Monster™ buckle. The US MOLLE II Waist Pack is listed under NSN 8465-01-465-2058, or enter WAIST PACK STYLE 4295 on an internet search engine.

C) US ALICE Waterproof Bag Liner (1 for ALICE Medium Rucksack): The waterproof bag liner was used early in the US Medium ALICE existence system as standard equipment. When the LC-2 Medium ALICE was adopted, the waterproof liner bag was given a separate NSN listing of 8465-00-258-2432. This bag provides roughly 1,500 cubic inches of space and fits inside the main compartment of the Medium ALICE rucksack. This rubber lined bag has a drawstring top, and it provides a waterproof interior for a Medium ALICE ruck. In the MH ALICE build, this component is optional.

MH ALICE Components:
OPTIONAL *(SUGGESTED BUT FLEXIBLE)* CONTINUED

D) SEAL gasket dry bag (for Sleep Carrier System or other): These dry bags are manufactured by SEAL LINE® in the commercial market and occasionally show up in surplus sales, since they are used in specialized contracts and sales to the US Navy. The SEAL LINE® dry bag is basically a heavy duty dry bag with a gasket compression seal. The military surplus SEAL LINE® bags are incredibly robust and are usually brown (coyote) in color. In the MH ALICE build, the large (3,150 cubic inch) bag is used as a compression bag for the Sleep System of choice to be stowed in the Sleep Carrier System. The gasket seal allows air to escape when compressed. Large, bulky, or lightweight items can be compressed to 25% of their normal size in these bags. Everything you need to know about this dry bag can currently be found at www.seallinegear.com/dry-bags. When doing an internet search, use: SEAL LINE DRY BAG MILITARY.

A NOTE ON NSN NUMBERS

National (or NATO) Stocking Numbers are used by the US Government and our NATO allies as a means of indexing all usable items in their inventories. By using the provided NSN numbers, you will be able to find many of the components needed for your MH ALICE build. Unless otherwise noted, the NSN numbers provided are for BDU (Woodland) camouflage units. Any popular internet search engine should be able to direct you to the proper surplus or private sale market for these items. When searching using the NSN numbers, be sure to place "NSN" before the number in your search.

MH ALICE TOTALS
IN CUBIC INCHES

The Basic MH ALICE build provides roughly 5,435 cubic inches of load-bearing capability: (Medium ALICE rucksack + US MOLLE II Sleep Carrier System).

The Deluxe MH ALICE build provides 6,564 cubic inches of load-bearing capability: (Medium ALICE rucksack + US MOLLE II Sleep Carrier System + US Field Training Pack + US MOLLE II Medical Pouch + US MOLLE II SAW Pouch -or- US General Purpose Large Pouch + Spec-Ops Brand H.U.M.P. Hydration Carrier). The addition of 1 US MOLLE II Waist Pack (as an optional unit) to the Deluxe MH ALICE would increase the load-bearing capability to 7,032 cubic inches.

In the NONCON system, some items may need to be stowed in a static location for future use. If you were to separate every component from the Deluxe MH ALICE build, along with all the optional components, the available cubic inches would be as follows (by component):

Medium ALICE Rucksack- 2,635

US MOLLE II Sleep Carrier System- 2,800

US Field Training Pack- 672

US MOLLE II Medical Pouch- 137

US MOLLE II SAW Pouch -or-
1 US General Purpose Large Pouch- 137

Spec-Ops Brand H.U.M.P. Hydration Carrier- 183

US MOLLE II Sustainment Pouches (900)- 1,800

US MOLLE II Waist Pack- 468

US ALICE Waterproof Bag Liner- 1,500

SEAL gasket dry bag- 3150

Total Cubic inches for NONCON use: 13,482

Again, this is a total of cubic inches available in the Deluxe MH ALICE build along with all the optional components for the NONCON system. This is not necessarily a cubic inch total for load-bearing needs. MH ALICE builds are flexible, so these components are just a recommendation based on an average build.

Photo credit Jesse Alphin

10/7/18

Lucas,
    Let's get together
    and build some
    NONCON rucks!

        Your Cousin,
        Jen

    Jn. 17:17

ABOUT THE AUTHOR
JESSE ALPHIN

Jesse Alphin researches US Military, UK Military, and commercial expedition load-bearing systems. The MH ALICE rucksack's creation results from 7 years of historical and provisional study in ALICE rucksack modifications.

Currently, Jesse is the President of Tradehawker LLC, (www.tradehawker.com) which specializes in Day-bag, BUG bag, and NONCON builds, as well as components for subsistence. All bags and rucksacks are complete for immediate shipment or made to order.

Jesse is dedicated to helping others obtain their load-bearing system of choice through technical writing, teaching, supplying, and building bags/rucksacks.

Jesse can be reached at **admin@tradehawker.com**, as well as **Tradehawker LLC on Instagram**.

For those who are curious, my (Creek's) personal MH ALICE NONCON Pack is the MH ALICE Deluxe Build and weighs approximately 75-80 lbs. fully packed. I am 5' 11" and weigh 160 lbs. My standard 3-day Bug Out Bag weighs 35 pounds.

MH ALICE Basic Build (side view) and MH ALICE Deluxe Build (side view).

CHAPTER 2

THE NONCON
PACK STARTER KIT

I've divided my NONCON Pack and this manual into 12 categories of NON-CONSUMABLE tools. However, through extensive field testing, I've found it extremely challenging to immediately start procuring consumables during the first 24–48 hours of a survival scenario, while also accomplishing other important survival objectives. At the outset of a NONCON scenario, one must spend time traveling, choosing a shelter site, setting camp, finding water, looking for resources, establishing a trap line, etc. It's hard to secure consumables while these steps are taking place. Thus, I developed a small consumable starter kit to buy myself some time. This kit allows me to settle into an area and make a survival plan for securing other consumable resources. I will start this portion of the manual by detailing the items in my NONCON Pack Starter Kit.

1 Full 40-Ounce Stainless Steel Klean Kanteen and 1 Full 64-Ounce Hydration Bladder: 104 ounces is just over 3 liters of fresh drinking water. While I carry several other water collection/purification tools (detailed later), I don't want to worry about sourcing water for the first couple of days in a NONCON scenario. This is weight I wish I didn't need, but water is so critical that I can't justify not having enough for drinking and various other needs, including hygiene, at the outset of a NONCON survival situation. For those who live in a water-rich environment, this is an area where weight could be cut (if desired).

40-Ounce Stainless Steel Klean Kanteen and 1 Full 64-Ounce Hydration Bladder.

Creek filling Sawyer Mini Water Filter System in small stream.

Sawyer Mini Water Filter System: At only 2 ounces and a cost of $20, the Sawyer Mini can filter up to a whopping 100,000 gallons of water. Although I can't imagine needing to drink 100,000 gallons of water from the wild, this product is, nonetheless, a consumable that is included in my starter kit for harvesting potable water. Obviously, this item will be used well into a long-term wilderness living scenario. Other water-related products are detailed later in this manual.

16-Ounce Jar of Peanut Butter: Peanut butter is an easy open-and-eat meal that is packed with calories for energy. It is also great bait for almost every trap and fishing implement I will mention later. Once empty, the lightweight and waterproof plastic container will prove useful.

16-Ounce Jar of Peanut Butter.

Resealable bag(s) of Beef Jerky: Beef jerky is an outstanding food while on the move. It was popular with primitive cultures for good reasons. It's an excellent fuel that keeps the body moving and requires absolutely no maintenance. It's great to eat dry, re-hydrated in stews, or even dipped in peanut butter!

Homemade Beef Jerky (thanks MOM!).

One Block of 12 Datrex Ration Bars: These 200-calorie ration bars have a 5-year shelf life and contain wheat flour, vegetable shortening, cane sugar, water, coconut flavor, and salt. The taste is bearable, in my opinion, and they are an excellent source of compact survival nutrition.

High calorie Datrex ration bars.

250 Count Tin of .22 caliber Air Gun Pellets: As you'll read later, my NONCON firearm is a .22 caliber air pellet pistol. At only a few ounces, this is my starting load of ammunition for this small game hunting tool.

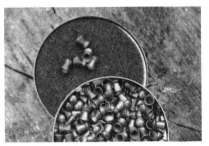

Small tin of .22 caliber air gun pellets.

Cleaning Wipes: Until a more permanent camp can be established, these wipes are perfect for cleaning the hands, face, tools, and they can even be used as toilet paper. I'd like to postpone using leaves and moss for as long as possible, but there just isn't space for more first aid or hygiene related paper goods than this in my NONCON Starter Kit.

Antibacterial cleaning wipes.

6 PET Balls and 1 Bic Lighter: If I need a fire during the first couple of days, I want it to be a no-brainer. Consequently, I pack a resealable bag with six cotton balls coated in petroleum jelly and one disposable Bic lighter. With these two items, fire is essentially guaranteed. As you'll learn later, my NONCON fire tools are quite different.

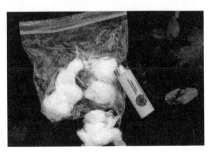

Six cotton balls saturated in petroleum jelly and one disposable lighter, both in resealable bags.

The previously mentioned items are all the consumables that I have in my pack. I stow these NONCON Starter Kit items in the US MOLLE II Sustainment Pouches (previously mentioned in Jesse's write-up). Everything else is a NONCON item and they are detailed in one of the upcoming 12 survival categories.

CHAPTER 3

SHELTER

My shelter strategy is two-fold: one is a shelter system for permanent/semi-permanent camps where I'll be remaining to gather consumables, and the other is a shelter system for when I'm between permanent/semi-permanent camps.

SHELTER SYSTEM FOR BETWEEN SEMI-PERMANENT CAMPS

Making camp with **NONCON** tent.

2 Person Camouflage Tent: There are many different tents of this variety that would work well. This one is light (3 lbs.) and of good construction. It is free-standing and doesn't require geographical anchor points, such as rocks or trees. If one of the tent poles breaks, saplings can be substituted. This is not the case with many other styles I considered. It has a mesh top for warm weather and a rain fly for inclement weather. I've used it many times and remain happy with this purchase. I can set it up in about 5 minutes and it straps easily to the exterior of my pack, above my sleep system. I chose the camo color for concealment. It can double as a gear cover if necessary. I chose a 2-person tent for extra interior room to house my gear. I actually purchased this tent at a yard sale, but similar styles can be found online.

BYER of Maine Mosquito Hammock: In my opinion, there is no use in having a hammock without a mosquito net canopy. This brand has served me well during many nights in the woods. It packs down to roughly the size of a grapefruit, and it is a very quick shelter deployment. It's hard to beat a hammock on sweltering hot nights. One of the tarps mentioned later can also be used as a canopy in inclement weather.

Making camp with **NONCON** hammock.

50 Feet 550 Paracord: This is cordage dedicated primarily to my hammock, though I could certainly cannibalize it for other needs. I've never needed more than 50 feet of cordage to set up my hammock.

Making camp with **NONCON** hammock.

NONCON SKILL

HOW TO TIE THE TWO BEST HAMMOCK KNOTS

Setting a hammock requires two knots—an anchor knot and a tensioning knot. I use the Timber Hitch for the anchor knot and the Trucker's Hitch for the tensioning knot. Below are step-by-step instructions detailing how to tie them.

Trucker's Hitch

To tie the Trucker's Hitch, start by forming an overhand loop on the standing part of the rope. Then, pull a bight from the working end up through the loop. This creates a slippery overhand loop. Next, run the working end around an anchor point, such as a tree. Note that pulling the working end too hard during this step will result in undoing the slippery overhand loop, so care must be taken here. The working end should then be run through the slippery loop, pulled tight, and then secured with two Half Hitches. Pinching the line on each side of the slippery overhand loop will allow for easier tying of the Half Hitches.

| Trucker Hitch: Step 1 | Trucker Hitch: Step 2 | Trucker Hitch: Step 3 |

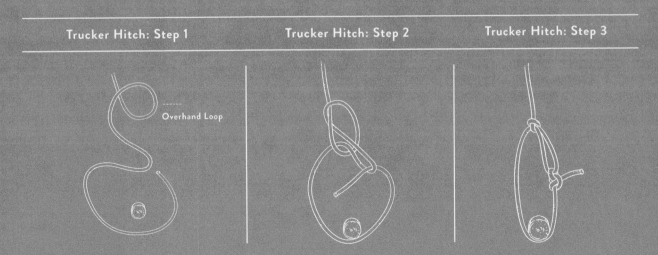

Overhand Loop

In a frictionless world, the design of the Trucker's Hitch allows for a 3 to 1 mechanical advantage when pulling a line tight. The physics of this mechanical advantage is what allows the user to pull the standing line so tightly between two objects. Due to friction through the loop and around the anchor point, the mechanical advantage isn't a true 3 to 1 ratio, but it's still enough to tighten with a force so impressive it can rival modern ratcheting straps.

Timber Hitch

The Timber Hitch is tied by first wrapping the rope around an object. Next, wrap the rope back around itself (the standing part), then twist it around itself three to five times. Finally, pull the rope tight to grip the object. While under strain, the Timber Hitch is very powerful. However, when the tension is released, it is very easy to untie. It can also be used to drag a log.

Timber Hitch: Step 1	Timber Hitch: Step 2	Timber Hitch: Set for dragging a log.

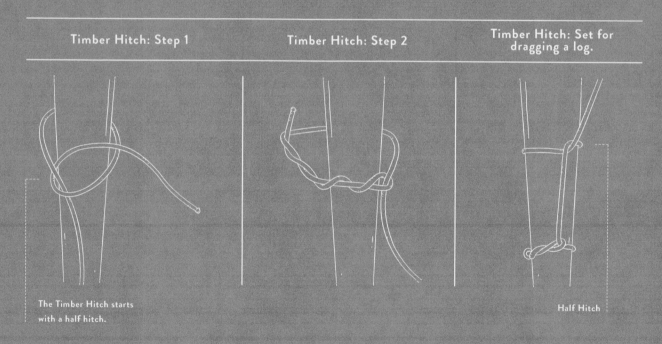

The Timber Hitch starts with a half hitch.

Half Hitch

SHELTER SYSTEM FOR SEMI-PERMANENT CAMPS

The semi-permanent shelter I have settled on for long-term living is one that I've used and tested many times. It is a hybrid shelter that utilizes both wilderness elements and tarps. I have provided detailed photographs of the completed shelter (above), and I have also included a step-by-step photo series documenting how to build it. It consists of a raised bush bed and a lean-to covered with a tarp (detailed later), and it is faced with an optional thick, clear vinyl front covering. The shelter framework was built using a 30" Bahco Bow Saw (detailed later) and paracord. Ideally, this shelter should be used when staying in one location for more than two weeks at a time.

Grabber All Weather Reflective Blanket: This 5'x7' tarp has a reflective side that provides an excellent back-wall when using a fire for warmth in cold weather environments. It is tied to shelter poles on the back side of the lean-to structure, using the grommets along its perimeter and paracord.

10'x10' Polyester Tarp: This is a tarp that can be purchased at nearly any hardware store. It's big and bulky, but it is also thick, durable, and waterproof. I own several of the thinner, lightweight bushcraft/camping tarps, and they just don't hold up after extended use. This tarp is draped over the back of the lean-to structure and secured with paracord. It will always be supported by a stick lean-to frame (as shown), thus suffering much less wear and tear with extended use.

8'x10' Clear Vinyl Tarp: I bought this on ebay.com for around $20. It is reinforced with the grid-work of a dental-floss-like fiber, which makes it very durable. As seen in the accompanying photos, this vinyl tarp is used in conjunction with the reflective back-wall to turn the entire lean-to shelter into a Mors Kochanski inspired Super Shelter. Radiant heat from the fire in front of the shelter passes through the clear vinyl front and is reflected down toward the sleeping bed where it is absorbed into the sleeping bags and body. The edges of the shelter are sealed off as best as possible, using brush and logs, to keep heat inside. The tarps and clear vinyl front also make the shelter waterproof and windproof. In warmer weather, when bugs and mosquitoes are an issue, a smoky smudge fire fueled by dry, rotting wood can be kept out front to produce enough smoke to keep the bugs away from the sleeping quarters. An optional lightweight mosquito net could be used for a covering as well. The clear front vinyl tarp is completely optional and can be rolled or folded away.

Note: I left this semi-permanent shelter system up from August through June in Central Indiana. I wanted to test the durability of the tarps, paracord, and general set-up over the harsh winter months. Through months of rain, snow and freezing cold temperatures, each of the listed components performed remarkably well. The inside of the shelter also remained bone dry.

NONCON SKILL

HOW TO BUILD CREEK'S SEMI-PERMANENT/ PERMANENT NONCON SHELTER

Below is a step-by-step photo series for how to build (what I believe to be) one of the most effective semi-permanent long-term wilderness living shelters.

The shelter starts with a strong, green ridgepole lashed between two trees with 550 paracord. Notice the load-bearing poles under it on each end.

Ridgepole is lashed to trees using paracord and the Square Lashing.

The raised bed frame is positioned about one foot back from the ridgepole.

A raised bed is built by stacking logs "log cabin-style" to a height of at least 12 inches above the ground.

Notice the two movable supports positioned at the hip and shoulder locations. These can be adjusted for comfort once the natural bedding is placed.

Flexible saplings (Willow shown here) are placed lengthwise to provide the flexible box frame for the sleeping area. The portions of the saplings with a thicker diameter are placed at the torso.

Leafy branch tips (1–2 feet) or evergreen boughs are placed, overlapping at a 45-degree angle, with tips facing inward and broken ends facing outward. These provide a cushioned mattress for sleeping. Use extras where hips and shoulders will be, as these are the areas that bear most of the weight.

Sleeping pad is placed on top of bed for comfort.

Sturdy limbs or trees are leaned against the ridgepole to form the lean-to back-wall framework. These should be long enough so they do not rest against the raised bed.

Smaller horizontal branches are lashed to the vertical poles to create a checkerboard framework of sticks that will adequately support the tarp.

10'x10' tarp lashed to shelter back-wall.

Lightweight logs leaned against tarp to hold it down during high winds.

Clear vinyl front wall lashed to front top of lean-to wall.

Side walls built with fallen logs and chinked with dead grasses.

Grabber reflective blanket lashed to inside of shelter back-wall for reflective heat from fire in front of the shelter. Notice a center ridgepole support pole has been installed as well.

Enjoying a nice shelter after several hours of work.

Front clear vinyl wall allows radiant heat from fire to pass through. This heat is reflected onto sleeping area from Grabber blanket on the inside of the shelter back-wall.

CHAPTER 4

SLEEP SYSTEM AND COMPONENTS

4-Piece Modular Military Sleep System: I've tested more sleep systems than I could ever count. Although this system certainly isn't the lightest, I have found it to be the most flexible for nearly any weather condition. Using this system, I've slept in just about every environment you can think of, including in the Sonoran Desert and high in the snow-laden Smoky Mountains. I've slept many nights beneath the stars with no shelter, using only this system, and I have woken in the morning to find myself dry and comfortable amid morning dew, snowfall, and even light rain.

The 4-piece system consists of a stuff sack, an outer Gore-Tex bivy bag, a green warm weather patrol sleeping bag and a black intermediate sleeping bag. Each of the bags can be used separately or combined for a sleep system rated to -30°F. Unlike natural goose down insulation, the synthetic polyester fill is quick to dry and holds its shape well with continued use. The Gore-Tex Bivy Bag has kept my body completely dry, even while sleeping during light rainfall, directly on top of deep snow, using only pine boughs as a sleeping pad.

At the time of this writing, this sleep system is available (new and used), through a variety of retailers, for as little as $89. It is a great system at an affordable price, considering that many bags with a similar rating can cost upwards of $400.

4-piece sleep system (from left to right): waterproof outer bivy sack, black intermediate bag, OD green warm weather patrol bag (stuff sack not shown).

Foam Reflective Sleeping Pad: I would never consider an inflatable pad for long-term wilderness living. A roll-up foam sleeping pad is larger, bulkier, and heavier, but it is MUCH more durable and can be used, in a variety of ways, for sitting and relaxing around camp. I purchased one with a reflective side from http://www.rothco.com that not only reflects body heat but can also double as a reflective wall in cold weather scenarios (like the Grabber tarp detailed previously).

Reflective foam sleeping pad.

CHAPTER

5

CLOTHING

Clothing proved to be one of the most difficult categories to manage in terms of space and weight. My strategy with clothing is less bulk and more layers, although many of the outer items I've chosen to take are very heavy and durable. Below is the complete list. Ordering links are made available at **http://www.creekstewart.com/noncon-list** where applicable. These items are IN ADDITION to what I will be wearing on my person (except for the Sundowner Hiking Boots).

- **Vinyl Poncho:** A rain poncho is critical.

- **Two Smartwool merino wool long sleeve base-layer tops**

- **Two Smartwool merino wool base layer bottoms**

- **Three Skivvy Rolls:** Each include a merino wool t-shirt, merino wool underwear, and a pair of Smartwool hiking socks (see NONCON Skill tutorial next).

- **Vasque Sundowner Boots (not in pack):** I wore the same pair of Vasque Sundowner Boots for 15 years straight, until I finally had to send them off to have the sole replaced. These boots are incredible. Animal fat or beeswax can be used in the field to both treat and waterproof the leather and seams.

> **Creek's favorite hiking boot: The Vasque Sundowner.**

- **Cheap foam-soled flip-flops for letting feet breathe around camp**

- **One pair of ALL RUBBER boots.** There is no cloth on these anywhere. They are shin-high rubber boots that I purchased at Tractor Supply. These are heavy, but they are durable and functional in the woods. They'll never fall apart or rot and are comfortable for day hiking excursions. A pair of neoprene Muck Boots would be a good option as well.

- **One mid-weight wool shirt-jac**

- **One mid-weight long sleeve fleece shirt**

- **A pair of bird hunting brush pants.** I've found this style of pants to be fantastic for spending time in the woods. The double layer of reinforcement on the front and back of the legs makes them incredibly durable.

Creek's brush pants (Eddie Bauer).

- **Gore-Tex pants** (waterproof, windproof shell for layering)
- **Hooded waterproof, windproof jacket** (shell for layering)
- **Fingerless wool gloves**
- **Mechanix M-PACT Gloves**

Mechanix M-PACT gloves for protecting hands.

- **Fleece beanie hat**
- **One merino wool neck gaiter**
- **Sunglasses/Safety Glasses** (1 pair)

Safety glasses for eye protection.

Clothing, by far, takes up the most space in my pack. However, clothing is often underestimated in its importance. Exposure to the elements is one of the greatest outdoor threats for someone trying to survive, and clothing is their first line of defense. For decades, I have studied survival stories and scenarios. A staggering number of these real-life situations could have seen better outcomes if those involved had been properly dressed for the environment in which they found themselves stranded or lost.

NONCON SKILL

THE SKIVVY ROLL

The Skivvy Roll is a great way to pack a clean set of the basics—t-shirt, underwear, and socks. Below is a photo series detailing how to make one.

STEP 1

STEP 2

STEP 3

STEP 4

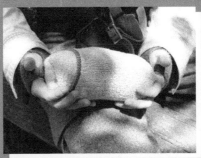

STEP 5

CHAPTER 5

WATER

Klean Kanteen in fire to boil water.

As mentioned earlier, a Sawyer Mini Water Filter System is in my NONCON Starter Kit. It is good for filtering up to 100,000 gallons of water. It comes with a 16-ounce reusable plastic pouch and a reusable drinking straw. Should I reach the 100,000 gallon limit, I have also packed my stainless steel Kelly Kettle stove kit for boiling water. It is by far the most efficient water boiling system I have ever used. With just a handful of twigs, I can bring several cups of water to a boil quickly. As I will detail under the upcoming COOKING category, The Kelly Kettle is also a very compact cook system. My 40-ounce stainless steel Klean Kanteen, is an additional container for boiling water.

In addition to the aforementioned materials, I also have the following items for harvesting, storing, and transporting water:

Harvesting rain water with Tarp Drain Kit.

Tarp Drain: This is a product I developed for one of my water-themed APOCABOXes, and it is now available to the public. It is a small plastic kit that allows a drain hole and hose to be placed in the middle of a tarp. The tarp can then be strung between trees during periods of heavy rain to harvest rainwater, which doesn't require purification. To collect the water, I have packed a 5-liter dry bag that I can suspend under the tarp with a tripod. The hose runs into the bag and the tripod holds the bag upright while it fills. I also pack an extra 5-liter dry bag to transport, collect, or store more water if necessary. These bags also make great water totes for carrying water from a nearby stream, pond, or seep back to camp. I have a 60"x 60" 70-denier rip stop nylon tarp dedicated to this harvesting system that I made from fabric purchased from an Amazon online seller. I had a local sign shop install grommets around the perimeter for stringing.

Improvised carved spile used to tap Sugar Maple tree.

Spile (QTY 3): Because they are so lightweight and take up virtually no space, I have also packed three spiles for tapping trees. One mature Maple can deliver up to several gallons of fresh drinking sap per day during late winter and early spring. This sap is not only drinkable straight from the tree, but it is also filled with vitamins, minerals, and nutrients. It can also be boiled down to a sugary drink or even syrup if desired. Other trees that can be tapped for drinking sap include Birch, Sycamore, and Basswood. This is an effortless way to get water during the right time of year and it can be collected in dry bags, metal canteens, or even folded bark containers.

Three metal spiles for tapping trees.

Creek with folded Eastern White Pine bark containers (a skill taught through http://www.survivalskillofthemonth.com).

NONCON SKILL

HOW TO IDENTIFY SUGAR MAPLE (ACER SACCHARUM)

The Sugar Maple is a deciduous tree, meaning it loses its leaves in the winter. The leaf has five lobes, like other Maple varieties. The two lobes on the bottom are much smaller than the three on the top. The big difference between the leaves of the Sugar Maple and other Maple varieties, such as the Silver Maple, are the sinuses (the deep notches in between the lobes). With Sugar Maples, these sinuses are rounded, as opposed to sharp (shown in the photo). Notice also how the leaf lobes have a very square shape. This is also indicative of the Sugar Maple.

Sugar Maple Leaf (fall season).

CHAPTER 7

FIRE

I'm convinced that fire is the most important survival skill. With the right tools, fire can be very simple. The tools I carry in my NONCON pack are detailed below.

Creek starting natural tinder (bark fibers) using shower of sparks from the Whiskey Ferro Rod.

Whiskey Ferro Rod: This is my proprietary Ferro Rod that I developed a while back. I pack it because I have started hundreds of fires with it and I KNOW it works. Measuring five inches long and a half-inch in diameter, it's also good for countless strikes with no fear of it running out. It is technically a consumable item, however, it will last me a lifetime of use. Although it has a recessed magnetic striker in the handle, I have attached an additional striker from Zombie Tinder that I like. It's their FERROSTRIKE, and it throws sparks like crazy. It can be found at: http://zombietinder.com/. This ferro rod is the only fire-starting device I will ever need. This particular ferro rod is available at http://www.creekstewart.com, however, there many other ferro rods with larger diameters that will work just as well for a NONCON scenario.

Char Kit: For tinder, I plan on using charred natural materials. To accomplish this, I've packed a 4" diameter x 1" deep circular tin for creating charred materials. I store this tin in a small canvas bag that also houses a resealable bag stuffed with charred cloth. As I run out of the char cloth tinder, I will replace it with charred punky wood, which is my natural charred tinder of choice. The metal tin is not waterproof, which is why I utilize the resealable bag.

NONCON SKILL

HOW TO CHAR PUNKY WOOD

Punky wood before charring.

Char tin placed into fire.

Punky wood ember, ignited using solar lens.

Punky wood is dry, rotting wood that can be crumbled into a powder between the fingertips. It is my natural char material of choice because it holds together well after being charred, and it is easy to convert into an ember for blowing a tinder bundle into flame. To make charred punky wood, fill a metal tin (like the one pictured) with large chunks of punky wood. DO NOT crumble it. Next, place this tin into the coals or flames of a fire. After roughly 30 seconds, you will notice smoke (and maybe some flames) exiting from the seam of the tin. This is the volatile gases escaping and burning as the punky wood is going through pyrolysis (the chemical change of organic matter by heat in the absence of oxygen). After the smoke and/or flames stop sputtering from the seam of the tin lid (approximately 3 minutes), carefully remove the red-hot tin with a stick or tongs and let cool. The contents will now be a carbonized version of punky wood that will readily smolder with a small spark from a ferro rod or a focal point from a solar lens. Small pieces of this charred wood can be made to smolder and then placed into a prepared tinder bundle, which can then be blown into flame.

Creek using 8.5" x 11" Fresnel Lens to ignite birch bark. This is an extremely powerful lens.

8.5" x 11" Solar Fire Starting Fresnel Lens: Why use a ferro rod when the sun is out? This 8.5" x 11" solar fire-starting Fresnel Lens is an incredible tool. I can't believe how powerful it is. These are available across the internet and at http://www.creekstewart.com.

2.5" x 3" Solar Fire Starting Fresnel Lens (QTY 5): I love these little magnifiers. They're lightweight and incredibly effective for establishing embers in full sun. I have packed one of these under the sole of each of my hiking boots for years. I also keep three in my fire kit for good luck.

Fire Scratcher: This is a fire-working tool that I've found to be very handy around camp. It's an extendable metal back scratcher that's been repurposed into a useful fire bellows, coal manipulator, pot grabber, etc. These can be found online or in many gas stations and pharmacies for only a few bucks. I find myself using it at camp to fiddle around in the fire more than I ever thought possible.

Creek using business card size magnifying lens to create an ember with punky wood.
GET ONE FOR FREE at:
http://www.creekstewart.com/free-tool

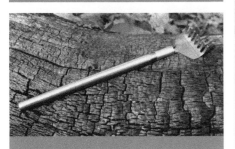

Close up shot of fire scratcher.

Creek using fire scratcher as bellows.

NONCON SKILL

MAKING A WOODEN COAL-BURNED CONTAINER

"I have a metal pot in my NONCON pack—I'll never need to know how to make a wooden coal-burned container!" These are what I like to call "famous last words." Metal pots are commonplace around the home and most people take them for granted. They are a nearly irreplaceable luxury in the woods. However, many cultures did and still do cook and boil water in wooden containers using hot stones. Native Americans were masters at using fire-heated stones to boil meats and stews in coal-burned wooden containers. I have also watched a group of men from the Middle East boil and cook a full-sized goat in a plastic drum, using only water and hot rocks. Many forms of modern Japanese cooking utilize hot rocks. Boiling takes more time with stones than it would with metal cookware, but it is possible. Stone boiling fosters a unique and intimate cooking experience. It's also a good skill to know because you never know when you might need it. Once the wooden container is made, hot rocks from the fire can be used to boil water or make stews. Below is a photo series depicting how to coal-burn a small container. The process is the same for larger bowls and cavities—even for coal-burned CANOES!

NOTE: *During the coal burning process, wet mud or clay can be used to prevent burning in certain areas. For example, if one side of the bowl cavity is burning faster than the other and you want to stop it or slow it down, simply press a layer of wet mud or clay over it.*

1) Start by carving a small cavity into the middle of a log or split log as shown.

2) Place a small, red-hot coal from the fire into the carved cavity. It should be just about the same size as the cavity itself. Use a long, hollow tube (the Fire Scratcher works perfect for this) to blow onto the red-hot coal and drive the "burn" into the surrounding wood. You will see it start to char and smolder. The cavity will slowly burn larger and larger. As it does, replace the coal with larger (and more) coals to increase heat and keep blowing.

3) Every so often, dump the hot coals out of the cavity and scrape the black charred areas around the cavity out with a sharp rock or knife. This will make the process of coal burning go much faster. I typically do three coal burning cycles to every one scraping cycle.

4) Once the cavity has reached the desired size, scrape the inside one more time to remove all of the charred wood and fill with water to see if there are any leaks. Cracks can be filled with clay or pine resin.

5) Red-hot rocks from a fire can be used to boil water or simmer stews in coal-burned wooden containers.

FIRE is truly the definitive survival skill. The ability to start a fire with limited tools, under the worst of conditions, is a skill that oftentimes makes the difference between life and death in a survival situation. If there is one survival skill worth mastering, it is FIRE. I'd like to invite you to take your fire-starting skills to the next level by training with me in my most extensive fire teaching series yet! It's called The Art of Fire. Enroll today at **creekstewart.com/artoffire.**

CHAPTER

8

Wild Edible Plant
OF THE MONTH CLUB

FORAGING

Wild Edible Plant of the Month Club Field Binder (http://www.wildedibleplantofthemonth.com).

Wild edibles include things like berries, nuts, leaves, stalks, seeds, barks, greens, fruits, and tubers. Gathering these items requires some kind of basket or bag, a trowel (for tubers), and knowledge (the most critical part). Unless someone has mastered the subject of wild edibles, they should carry a field guide for reference. One great option is the Peterson Field Guide to Edible Wild Plants of Eastern/Central North America. Even if you live in a western state, this is still a very useful and applicable guide, as many of the plants listed are also found in the west. Although the guide is illustrated with black and white line art, it includes key descriptive features and illustrations that are incredibly accurate and insightful. If you're interested in expanding your wild edible plant knowledge, consider subscribing to my Wild Edible Plant of the Month Club starting at only $4.99/month at **http://www.wildedibleplantofthemonth.com.** I cover a new wild edible plant each month in unprecedented detail with multi-season macro-photography and descriptive text about harvesting and preparation. By focusing on only one plant each month, you will gradually master some of the world's most popular wild edible plants. In addition to the Peterson's field guide, there are a few other items in my pack to help with foraging food from wild plants and trees. I have listed them on the following pages.

Creek's personal copy of Peterson Field Guide to Edible Wild Plants of Eastern/Central North America.

Foraging Knife: Some may consider this tool to be unnecessary weight for a NONCON pack, but a compact trowel, like this one, can speed up the foraging process, especially when digging for roots and tubers, such as Wild Leeks or Chufa. This trowel is not only a sharp mini-shovel, but it also has sharpened edges for cutting roots and barks. Over time, this tool will save some wear and tear on your main survival knife, and it outperforms a traditional digging stick.

Foraging knife that doubles as handy trowel.

NONCON SKILL

IDENTIFYING AND HARVESTING CHUFA
(*CYPERUS ESCULENTUS*)

Dried Chufa tubers.

Characteristic Chufa seed head.

Some of my research suggests that Chufa (also called Yellow Nutsedge) tubers could represent an impressive percentage of the diet for our primitive ancestors in North America. Other names for Chufa tubers are Earth Almond and Tigernuts. Chufa grows around water and in low areas, typically in full sun. It is prevalent in almost every region, except for arid desert environments. It is such an unappreciated edible plant resource, and it produces one of my absolute favorite wild foods. Chufa grows many edible nut-like tubers that are ready to harvest in the fall. These sweet, almond-flavored tubers (rarely larger than the diameter of a dime) grow at the end of the spindly roots. After they're washed, they can be eaten raw, dried, boiled as a side, or mixed in soups and stews. They dry wonderfully on a rack (detailed later) and can be kept for food all winter. If setting up a long-term camp, Chufa also makes a perfect crop for a survival garden. These tubers also make excellent bait for turkey, deer, fish, carp, ducks, and any animals that live near water. The only catch with Chufa is that the tubers only grow plentifully in soil that is sandy or loamy. They are hard to find (and often tiny) in soil that is hard and packed with clay. For a survival crop, mixing sand from a nearby creek or stream with planting soil can produce good results.

Creek stuffing Lamb's Quarters wild greens into recycled orange bag.

Mesh Bags: I've packed a few sizes of simple, cheap, and lightweight mesh bags for foraging things like leaves, greens, and mushrooms. One of these is a bag that originally contained sweet corn from a local farmer's market. The others are Coghlan's Brand and cost under $5 for three on Amazon. They don't have to be fancy. These mesh bags can also be used for carrying fish, trapped game, crayfish, birds, or any other animals you may be able to harvest (mentioned in FISHING and TRAPPING categories). They can also be hung in full sun or over a smudge fire for drying herbs and mushrooms.

Homemade Screen Drying Rack (QTY 4): I'm a big fan of drying extra fruits, roots, tubers, seeds, and berries so they can be stored through the winter or even carried on the trail. One way to make this process easier is by using a screen drying rack. To build the rack, I purchased a 24"x 24" section of window screen material and had a sign shop put a few grommets around the perimeter so that I could tie it to a tripod or quad-pod. This handy drying rack rolls up and stuffs into a very small space in my pack. It's made from fiberglass and does not crease or warp with folding. This can double as a sieve or strainer for other cooking functions as well. I will also use this for drying jerky over a smudge fire (detailed later).

Variety of edibles drying in the sun on homemade drying screens.

NOTE: *Any of the containers mentioned throughout other categories would make perfect containers for collecting nuts, fruits, and berries, should the opportunity arise. Another option would be to source trash containers that have been littered around, as I'm sure there will be no lack of them.*

NONCON SKILL

HOW TO MAKE A FOLDED PINE BARK CONTAINER

Bark containers were very popular among primitive cultures for foraging and storing goods. In the spring, when the sap is running, many different tree barks readily peel from the heartwood and can be fashioned into folded bark containers. My favorite tree bark to use for a quick and dirty folded bark container is from the Eastern White Pine. See the photo series below for instructions on how to fashion a box-shaped container, using a square or rectangular piece of freshly peeled Pine bark.

Pinch the corner as shown.

Fold pinched corner inward.

Pin corner into place with split stick tied at top to prevent splitting through.

Finished pinned side.

Finishing final corner of completed bark container.

Learn unique survival skills like this one at http://www.survivalskillofthemonth.com

CHAPTER 9

FISHING

(AND OTHER ANIMALS/REPTILES FOUND AROUND WATERWAYS)

Where I live, in Central Indiana, fish (and other animals/reptiles found around waterways) are one of the most readily available food sources. Every stream, pond, creek, and river abound with fish. Even small trickling creeks contain crayfish and minnows. A significant number of my food procurement kit items fall under this category. You'll notice, in this category and in the HUNTING category, that I included very few tools for ACTIVE hunting and fishing. This is because I believe (for me at least) that I can harvest more food through passive fishing and trapping than I can through active fishing and hunting. In my personal experience, the time invested in setting multiple fishing traps or animal traps versus actively fishing or hunting for the same quarry yields better results. My NONCON tools that fall under the FISHING category are listed on the following pages.

Creek gigging frog for food and bait.

Frog Gig: Even though frog gigging is active hunting, I have found it to be an easy way to get food during the summer months. As long as a flashlight with charged batteries (detailed under the MISCELLANEOUS category) is available, frog gigging almost always yields good results for me. Also, I like frog legs.

NOTE: *Leftover frog heads and bodies also make incredible bait for trotlines and leg-hold traps. This gig can also be used to take fish at night or while spawning at the water's edge. Included with this gig are a couple of wood screws, which I use to secure it to the end of a locally sourced sapling. These items are all kept together in a cloth drawstring bag.*

Frog gig fixed to end of gig pole using wood screw (screwed in with Leatherman MUT Multi-tool).

Grilled frog legs on makeshift cross-cut wooden plate, garnished with tart Yellow Wood Sorrel.

Monofilament Line: I carry two spools of monofilament line in 20 LB test. Bluegills, pan fish, and sun fish are by far the easiest fish to catch in my region. They can be caught with a makeshift fishing rod fashioned from a cane pole, a 10-foot piece of monofilament line, a hook, locally sourced live bait, a sinker, and a bobber.

Two spools of monofilament fishing line.

Micro Pocket Fishing Rod & Reel: There are a variety of these available on Amazon for under $15. For the price and size, they are a great little kit addition, and I've pulled in some bass, crappie, and perch much larger than the rod & reel itself! This little combo also gives the option for spin casting.

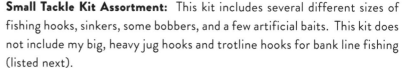

Micro Pocket Reel in Creek's hand.

Small Tackle Kit Assortment: This kit includes several different sizes of fishing hooks, sinkers, some bobbers, and a few artificial baits. This kit does not include my big, heavy jug hooks and trotline hooks for bank line fishing (listed next).

NOTE: *Fishing hooks can be used to catch a host of critters in a survival scenario. A duck trap can be quickly fashioned by anchoring several hooked lines to a board or log and baiting them with corn, berries, or plant tubers (such as Chufa). This can be placed on the shore and checked daily where duck activity has been observed. Turkey can also be caught using hooks in a similar fashion. They are especially fond of Chufa tubers. Only do this in a LIFE or DEATH survival scenario.*

Small NONCON Fishing Kit.

EZ Trotline Kit: I included this kit in the BUSHCRAFT DUMP POUCH Edition of the APOCABOX. It is a simple kit that includes the following items:

- **150' of #18 tarred nylon line on a 6" reusable plastic tube**
- **20 of size 2/0 hooks (inside the plastic tube)**
- **Plastic plugs in each end of the plastic tube**
- **Directions on how to put hooks on line**

EZ Trotline Kit.

This kit allows me to quickly and easily set a long trotline, up to 20 bank lines, or up to 20 jug sets along the edges of creeks, streams, or ponds. These lines are perfect for catching catfish, carp, turtle, and even small alligator. I'm a big fan of trotlines and bank lines for many reasons, but my top three are: 1) They work 24/7, like a snare. 2) The bait can be any kind of animal leftovers, such as a frog head or fish guts. 3) They are very inconspicuous and almost impossible to see from the shore, unless you know exactly where they are (trap theft can be an issue).

NONCON
SKILL

HOW TO TIE THE IMPROVED CLINCH KNOT
FOR ATTACHING HOOK TO LINE

I use the Improved Clinch Knot almost exclusively for tying fishing hooks to monofilament and tarred line.

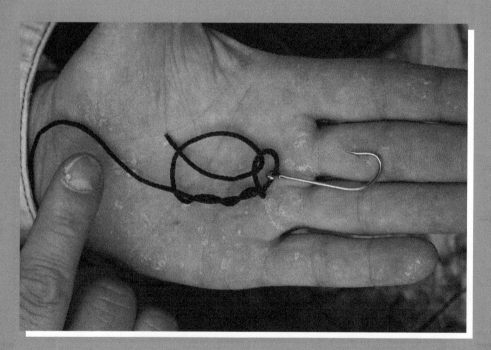

Photo of Improved Clinch Knot, using #18 tarred trotline.

MAGIC BAIT Economy Trotline Kit: This line is 100 feet long and has little metal rings evenly spaced throughout for attaching head clips, drop lines, and hooks. The 25 size 4/0 hooks included in the kit are great for catfish, carp, and turtle.

Magic Bait Trotline Kit (left) and assembly of clips and hooks (below).

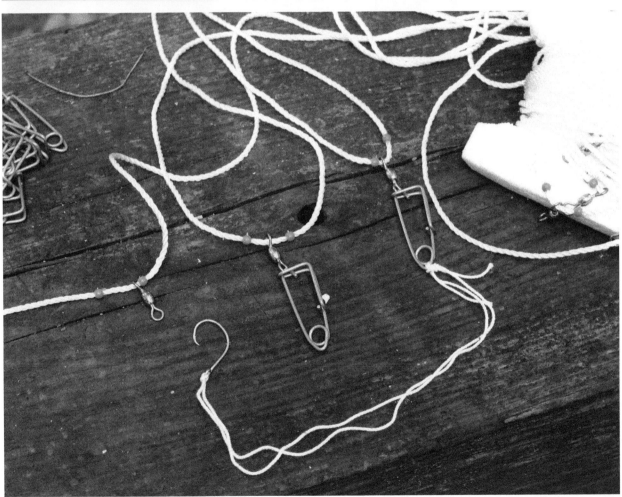

NONCON KNOWLEDGE

UNDERSTANDING DIFFERENT FISHING SET LINES

"Set Line" is a generic term used to describe a variety of different passive fishing methods. Below is a description of several line types that I will employ in a NONCON survival scenario.

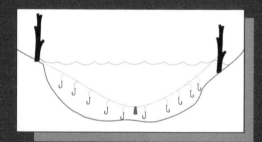

Trotline: A trotline is a long, thick line (I use tarred nylon with a minimum test of 100 lbs.) that has baited hooks spread evenly across its length. The hooks are attached to smaller lines, called snoods, and they are typically tied onto barrel swivels, which are tied onto the main line. I almost always make my snoods about 12" long. I've found that if they are any longer, they get tangled around the main line too much. I use metal clips to hold my snoods onto the barrel swivels. Trotlines are typically set across a body of water, such as a stream or river. I suggest tying off both ends to a root or anchor point slightly under the water line so that no one sees the line and steals it. Once the line is stretched across the water, it can be weighted so that it sinks toward the bottom where the target fish (catfish) spend their time. The snood hooks must be baited well. I typically bait with other parts of fish (heads/tails), frogs, guts, and scraps from other kills. A seine (detailed later) will come in handy for snagging good bait, too. Whatever you bait with, make sure the hook sinks into it well. Setting the line is easier with a boat, but it can be thrown across the water using a weight. Throwing the line will limit how long your line can be, thus, limiting how many snoods are on it as well.

Bank Line: A bank line is basically the same concept as a trotline. However, one end is anchored to a tree or limb on the bank and the other end is attached to another anchor, such as a rock or piece of scrap metal to hold it down in the water. This type of set line is much easier to "toss" in from the shore and can be shorter in length. It can even be a single baited hook.

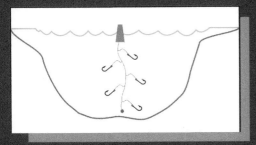

Drop Line: A drop line is essentially a trotline, except it is set vertically in the water, rather than horizontally across a body of water. A drop line is set into place with an anchor, and a float is used to mark it at the top of the water. I'll oftentimes bait my drop lines to target different fish at different depths—sunfish at top, crappie and bass in the middle, and catfish on the bottom. I typically float my drop lines with an empty 2-liter bottle or milk jug.

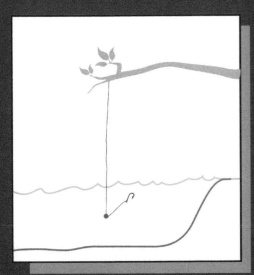

Limb Line: I've had much success with limb lines. These are single hook lines tied to limbs which overhang the body of water. The flexible limbs help to tire the fish, as they provide resistance. Movement of these limbs is a good indicator that there is a fish on the hook. I make my limb lines the same way every time. I tie a loop knot about 12" up from the baited hook end. Then, I attach a weight onto the loop. On the limb end, I tie another fixed loop using an overhand knot, then wrap this loop around the limb and drop the hook and sinker through it. Then pull tight to secure.

Jug Line: A jug line is like a limb line with the exception that the line is attached to a floating plastic container. I typically use 2-liter bottles or milk jugs. I do not use jug lines in creeks and streams because they float downstream. I only use them in small ponds where I can easily keep track of them. I use the same setup for jug lines I do for the limb lines (mentioned in the section above).

Collapsible Bait Trap: Also included in my pack is a lightweight, collapsible bait trap that I had made exclusively for APOCABOX subscribers (http://www.myapocabox.com). It collapses down to 12"x12"x 2" and weighs only a few ounces. The attached bait bag makes catching minnows, crayfish, and other small fish very simple, and it is incredibly effective. Just fill the bait bag with crushed up insects and you'll always have a supply of live minnow bait for setting your fishing lines. This bait is perfect for using on all the set lines previously mentioned.

Collapsible minnow/bait trap (collapsed) and Creek tossing minnow trap into pond.

4' x 10' x 1/8" Douglas Minnow Seine: My grandpa, from Kentucky, taught me how to use a seine in small creeks and streams when I was just a kid. He would hold the seine in both hands, as wide as he could, and walk upstream for several yards. Then, he'd bring it to the shore to reveal a pot-luck assortment of minnows, crayfish, suckers, aquatic bugs, and the occasional snake. He would then toss these critters into a bucket to be used for bait later that day when we'd go fishing, oftentimes after cutting our own river cane fishing poles. While a bit heavy and bulky, this seine is unrivaled in its ability to quickly gather small aquatic critters. It also doubles as a net to catch larger fish when strung across narrow chokes in rivers, creeks, and streams.

Creek using seine just as his grandfather taught him.

QTY 6: Yo-Yo Fishing Snares: These little mechanical fishing yo-yos are fish-getting machines! If you're not familiar with them, they are basically a bank line that jerks back when it's triggered. As soon as the fish takes the bait, the trigger releases and the yo-yo sets the hook and applies constant tension on the line. They can be secured to a stake or tree on the shore. For the weight and price, these are a no-brainer for inclusion in any survival fishing kit. They are extremely effective.

Creek setting Yo-Yo fishing snare over river.

"IN MY PERSONAL EXPERIENCE, THE TIME INVESTED IN SETTING MULTIPLE FISHING TRAPS OR ANIMAL TRAPS VERSUS ACTIVELY FISHING OR HUNTING FOR THE SAME QUARRY YIELDS BETTER RESULTS."

CHAPTER
10

ACTIVE HUNTING

As mentioned earlier, I've decided not to include any active hunting gear, except for the item listed below (and the Frog/Fish gig mentioned earlier). I debated for quite some time about including a take-down bow and arrow but ultimately opted against it. Instead, I beefed up on trapping kit items (detailed in the TRAPPING section) because these tend to yield better results for me when I compare effort and time invested. However, I couldn't resist including my Crosman 2289 Backpacker Pellet Gun. It is detailed below.

Crosman 2289 Backpacker Pellet Gun.

Crosman 2289 Backpacker Pellet Gun: It's important to note **TWO** things. **First,** this model has been discontinued by Crosman. However, I will mention a current model (at the time of this writing) that's even better. **Second,** this gun has been modified with better parts and pieces to increase its pumping power and feet-per-second (and killing power). I'll detail the specifics of these upgrades momentarily. Before you start thinking that this gun is a CONSUMABLE item because it uses ammunition, I have also found a way around that issue.

I always think it's funny when I hear people say that pellet guns aren't good hunting guns. That just tells me that those individuals aren't good hunters. I've killed and eaten more small game animals with my assortment of .22 caliber pellet guns (I prefer the heavier .22 pellet over the .17 pellet) than I could ever detail in this manual. I've killed and eaten fish, frogs, snakes, turtles, rabbit, dove, pigeon, squirrel, chipmunk, pine squirrel, rat, and a huge variety of birds that are considered invasive and aren't otherwise protected. I've killed big Indiana Fox Squirrel with my 2289 Backpacker from 30 yards away. Birds are one of the most plentiful meat sources available in the wild, but they are also the hardest to catch—UNLESS you have a pellet gun. You can mound up a pile of birds large enough for a filling

meal in under 30 minutes (in survival scenario only, of course). Besides a .22 Long Rifle, a .22 caliber pellet gun that has been properly sighted-in and modified with more robust parts to be a little more powerful is one of my favorite small game hunting guns. Does it require you to stalk a little better? Yes. Does it require you to aim a little better? Yes. Does it require more patience and attention? Yes. However, when it comes to a .22 caliber pellet gun for a NONCON scenario, the benefits far outweigh the drawbacks. It's also nearly silent and weighs just a few pounds (that's including the gun and hundreds of pellets).

Creek with Red Fox Squirrel taken with 2289 Backpacker Pellet Gun from 30 yards.

As can be seen in the photo, the 2289 Backpacker is a pistol. It has an optional stock that can be screwed on, but I prefer the pistol configuration for size and weight. It fits perfectly in my pack and is very easy to maintain. It is a wonderful little gun, and when rested against a tree or on a forked stick, I can hold it dead steady. A very important feature of this gun is that it is a PUMP model. This means that you pump it up to provide the air pressure. In a survival scenario, this is a critical detail—otherwise you're dependent on CO2 cartridges or compressed air. This gun has a built-in pump for providing its own power.

Like I mentioned earlier, the model I carry is no longer available. Luckily, there are air gun enthusiasts, like http://www.alchemyairwerks.com/, that cater specifically to those needing something special. Alchemy makes and sells the 2289 Packman, which is a "built-from-ground-up", better version of the Backpacker model. They can also set you up with extra seals and any replacement parts that you might want to carry in your kit, just in case there is a failure after continued use. I will say that I've fired thousands of pellets from my Backpacker with no problems. Alchemy uses higher-end, more robust parts and pieces which add durability AND POWER to this little gun, allowing you to pump it more times per shot than a stock model. This isn't an "off-the-shelf" pellet gun. It's modified for real use in the field—not just plinking tin cans in the backyard (although that is fun).

As you can tell, I consider my 2289 Backpacker a real tool in my survival arsenal. It's proven to me, repeatedly, that it can deliver results. Regardless of what you hear about pellet guns from self-proclaimed "gun experts", they are real guns and can put real food on the table. Moreover, I know of no other gun that is as lightweight, takes up as little space, is quieter, is self-powered, and uses ammunition that can be made in the field over a campfire. That's right my friend, ammo made in the field...keep reading.

.22 Caliber NOMAD Pellet-Making Kit: I purchased this pellet-making kit from https://www.airgunpelletmaker.com/. These kits are all made by hand on a lathe. With this kit, you can mold your own pellets (5 at a time) in just a few minutes. Almost any kind of scrap lead can be melted down over the hot coals of a campfire and poured into this mold. Although scrap lead is getting harder to find (ask any hobby bullet caster), it is certainly still available. The best source I've found is lead wheel weights that tire shops use to balance tires. Just a few of those weights can make upwards of 50 pellets. Even though lead is no longer being used to make these weights, there are still many made of lead out there, and I come across them all the time. Used bullets from gun ranges also make perfect scrap lead for melting into pellets.

Lead fishing weights are also great candidates. Other soft metals may work as well, but I've never tried anything besides lead. Even used pellets recovered from inside small game animals you've already hunted can be remolded and reshaped using this kit. In theory, with this kit and some occasional scrap lead, you can have a never-ending supply of ammunition. The only other tool you need besides a hammer (I use the butt of my axe) is a melting ladle.

Lee Precision Lead Ladle: For under $6, this is the cheapest lead-melting ladle I could find. Just put in some scrap lead and place it directly on red hot coals (or over a small rocket stove) to melt the lead and pour it into your pellet mold.

Lee Precision Lead Ladle being used to melt down small lead scraps.

NOTE: *For the size and weight of lead .22 caliber pellets, one can also easily carry several thousand in a NONCON Pack. A supply of that volume can last for many years. There probably wouldn't be much difference in weight if you were to pack the pellet making kit and ladle, so it's certainly something to consider. It's not theoretically NONCON, but it may be your preference.*

NONCON SKILL

TIPS FOR MELTING SCRAP LEAD OVER A CAMPFIRE WITH A LEE PRECISION LEAD LADLE (OR SIMILAR)

Pouring melted lead into NOMAD Pellet Mold.

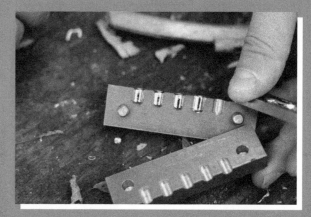

Freshly made pellets before final shaping.

Below are some basic tips for melting your own scrap lead over the coals of a fire in the field.

1. Melt on the coals, not the flame. Best results can be achieved by resting the ladle directly on a hot bed of coals.

2. Melting lead should take less than five minutes.

3. If possible, only melt lead outdoors and don't hover over it. It's never a good idea to inhale lead fumes.

4. Molten lead solidifies quickly, so get to pouring once it melts.

CHAPTER 11

TRAPPING

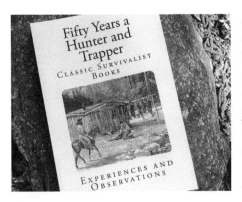

As I've mentioned previously, I'm banking most of my weight and space in my NONCON Pack for food procurement on trapping supplies. This stuff is heavy. That's just the nature of good, reliable trapping equipment. Any experienced trapper will tell you and agree with me when I say this: ***If you wait until you are in a survival scenario to use your trapping equipment, then you might as well not even have it—because it requires some experience.*** It's not difficult, but there are tips and tricks that you truly only learn after having set a few traps and caught a few animals. One of my favorite books on the subject is titled *Fifty Years a Hunter and Trapper* by E.N. Woodcock. Below are the trapping tools of the trade that I include in my NONCON Pack.

1.5 Coil Spring Trap ready to be bedded down at the entrance to a small game den.

QTY 6: 1.5 Coil Spring Traps: These are smaller and lighter than conibear-style traps but just as effective and less dangerous. A big difference is that these are live capture traps, so be prepared to club (or shoot) your quarry when checking the line. Coil spring traps are foothold traps, and I've found the 1.5 coil spring to be the best all-around trap, although I'm quickly becoming a fan of the 1.65 as well. The 1.5 has an open-jaw diameter of just under 5 inches, and it is easy to bed down and camouflage. It can function as a drowning trap on animals, such as mink and muskrat, but it can also capture and hold animals such as raccoon, fox, skunk, opossum, feral cats, and smaller dogs (even up to small coyotes). The pressure on the pan is usually adjustable with a screw if you wanted to dial it up or down to make it more or less sensitive. The brands I have and like are Duke and Bridger. **NOTE:** *I have decided not to pack stakes for securing these traps. I will either carve the stakes from wood or tether the traps to an anchor or drag.*

NONCON SKILL

HOW TO MAKE A CUBBY SET USING A 1.5 COIL SPRING TRAP

The Cubby Set is one of my most frequently used land methods for trapping raccoon and opossum, both of which are excellent survival meals. Below is a step-by-step photo series detailing how to properly make a Cubby Set.

The front of a small log cubby built up against a tree. A "cubby" is a little shelter made to house the bait and funnel a target animal.

The back of the cubby set.

The side of the cubby set. Notice the stakes used to help stack the logs into position for the sides.

I've used a new "unweathered" trap for the purposes of this photo series because it stands out better against the dirt. First, place the trap right in front of the cubby opening and draw an outline around it in the dirt. Clear away forest debris if necessary. The outline should be about 2 inches bigger than the trap.

Remove the trap and dig out the dirt on the inside of the outline so that the trap is flush with the ground when setting on the bottom of the dug-out cavity.

Side view of trap placed in dug-out cavity for reference.

Now, lightly sprinkle enough sand/dirt to barely cover the trap. Not too much.

Leave the pressure pan barely exposed, as can be seen in this photo.

The trap chain should be anchored to an immovable object, such as a tree or, in this case, a 24-inch stake driven deep into the ground using the back side of my hatchet.

Now, cover the chain with dirt and camouflage the area with typical forest debris.

Before leaving the area, place the bait into the back of the Cubby Set. The walls and roof of the cubby will funnel the animal through the front opening and across the disguised coil trap.

PREPARING YOUR TRAPS FOR THE FIELD

BY STEPHEN KINNEY

First, I cannot stress enough the importance of checking your local laws for trapping before going out to trap any animals using manufactured traps or snares.

I was introduced to the trapping world by my family members, in central North Carolina, at a young age. Like most teenagers, I thought I knew everything there was to know about everything, including trapping. How wrong I was. By the age of 15, I was setting several traps on my own, and I did get lucky from time to time. I stress the word "lucky". There are some procedures that need to be followed to give a trapper the best chances of catching their target animal. Over my years of experience as a trapper, I have learned what works best for success in the field. In the next few paragraphs, I will go over the steps that have worked for me, time and time again, whether I'm using traps or snares.

To begin, there are a few different types and sizes of traps. Most people begin with a simple foot trap (Coil Spring or Long Spring). Both operate in the same manner, as they use a spring-operated closure to close the jaws of the trap onto the leg of the target animal. In conjunction with these traps, they must be anchored to the ground by a "T" stake, ground anchor, or using wire to secure the end of the chain to a tree or stump. This will prevent the animal from escaping with the trap attached to its leg, which is not good for the animal or your success in obtaining the animal. Below are some basic guidelines that will really jumpstart your trapping knowledge.

1) **What are You Trapping:** Chose the correct size of trap you will be needing. Smaller animals, like fox or raccoon, use a #1.5 or #2 size trap. For larger animals, such as coyote, a #3 will do the trick. Between manuals and online research, there is a plethora of information for you to reference for trapping animals native to your area. This research will give you an idea of what animal(s) you should target. Once you have chosen your traps and purchased them (I suggest starting with 6 or so), it's time to get to work.

2) **Adjusting the Trap:** The first thing that needs to be done is setting the tension on the pan (the part of the trap on which the animal steps), this is accomplished by loosening or tightening the pan. It should take 1.5 pounds of pressure to move the pan. Because traps are mass produced, you'll find some require more effort to adjust the pan, while others take much less. When it comes to adjusting the tension, the pan should sit flat or horizontal once the trap is set. If the pan sits at an angle, it will require more force to trip, which could result in missing the animal altogether. The pan height is adjusted by filing the catch at the back of the pan. ONLY remove small bits at time. If too much is removed, your trap will not set properly. I have found that most quality traps are close to perfect straight from the factory.

Materials used to clean factory made traps: some pots and a propane burner.

3) Clean It Up: All traps are produced by machinery and have a coating of oil to prevent rusting. The oil is good for storage, but it is BAD for trapping. Animals have a heightened sense of smell and can easily pick up on the aroma of the oil, which keeps them away from your set trap. Removing the factory coating of oil from a trap is not difficult, but there is a specific process that needs to be followed. First, open the jaws of the trap and place a nail between the jaws to allow the cleaning solution to get to all parts of the trap. Get an old pot and put enough water in the pot to submerge all the traps you are cleaning. Also, add one quart of vinegar per gallon of water (a 4:1 ratio of water to vinegar). I prefer to add some dish soap to the pot as well (you'll see the reasoning for this momentarily). Bring the water to a boil, and adjust your heat to keep it at a boil for about fifteen minutes (at that point all the oil should be removed from your traps and boiled out of the pot). The dish soap helps draw the oil out of the pot, so when you retrieve the traps you aren't picking them up through the oil on top of the water. From this point on, **DO NOT** handle your trap with your bare hands! You will transfer oils and dirt onto the trap which will lessen your chances of catching an animal, and it will void all the work you've put into cleaning your traps thus far. Using a rod, stick, coat hanger, or bungee cord, remove the trap from the pot and rinse it off with clean water, then hang the trap up to let it dry. I use the same pot, year after year, just for cleaning my traps.

Nail placed between jaws to keep them slightly open.

Traps placed in cleaning solution to boil.

Removing trap from boiling solution after fifteen minutes.

Traps hanging on a line outside to rust.

Photo of trap AFTER rusting process.

Photo of trap AFTER dying process.

4) **Let It Rust:** I know this goes against everything you have learned about bare metal, but a thin coat of rust is required for the next step. Typically, it takes just a couple of days of hanging outside for a trap to collect a thin coating of rust. If you live in a place with very low humidity, spraying them with water a couple of times will help to speed up the rusting, or "weathering" process. Don't worry if the rust is uneven across the trap or snare. It's OK, the rust is necessary.

5) **Add Some Color:** Now that there is a light coating of rust on the trap, some color needs to be added and the rusting process slowed to make the trap less visible to an animal. There are several different manufactures of trap dye. Some use water and others use gas. I have used several different dyes over the years and have found that the dyes that are mixed with water preform the best. They are also easier to use, in my opinion. Longwood Trap Dye, which is produced by the Duke Co., is by far my favorite store-bought dye. Mix one pack of the powdered dye into five gallons of water. Warm the water to a point that it is steaming (not boiling), then dip your trap into the mixture. After a few minutes, the trap will reach the same temperature as the water. Remove the trap from the water at this point. If you have a good layer of rust for the dye to adhere to, it shouldn't take much to get a rich, dark color on your trap. Finally, hang the trap to dry. Afterward, you'll have yourself a dyed trap that is going to be less visible, even with a shallow set, and last for a whole season under normal use. I can dye a couple dozen of my traps/snares with just one dye package and five gallons of water

6) **Wax Your Trap:** Now that your trap is adjusted, cleaned, weathered, and dyed, it's time to protect your traps so they can provide you with years of service. There are a few companies that manufacture "trap wax" in large bars, which is what I use every season. The wax will prolong the life of your traps (I still use my grandfather's traps). There are 2 ways to wax your traps. I call them the "Indoor" and "Outdoor" methods.

Indoor Method: Using a large pot, place a couple of traps inside and add enough water to cover them. Then, remove the traps from the pot and start heating up the water. Next, add your wax to the pot and allow the wax to melt (water boils at 212°F, which is more than enough to melt the wax). Once the wax has melted, it will sit on top of the water (the wax and water do not mix). Dip your trap into the pot (using a hanger or hook) until it is completely submerged. Allow your trap to come up to the same temperature of the water. Next, take your trap out of the pot, and as the trap moves through the wax on top of the water, it will coat the trap entirely. This process allows for more wax to transfer to the trap. There's nothing wrong with that, but some "flaking" will occur. **Note:** *This is the safest way to wax your traps.*

Finished trap AFTER waxing process.

Outdoor Method: Using a propane burner, slowly heat up the wax in a pot until it is completely melted. The pot only needs to be big enough to fit one trap at a time, however, the pot should be deep enough that one trap can be completely submerged in the wax. Using a pot hanger or hook, dip your trap into the wax and allow it to warm up to the temperature of the wax (a couple of minutes is enough), then remove your trap and hang it to dry. This will put a thin coating of wax on your trap, which means you will not have much "flaking" at all. ***CAUTION: Wax will ignite on its own at just over 400°F, and a spark can ignite your wax once it has liquefied (if heating over open flame).*** I play it safe and always prepare for a wax fire, and you should, too. Treat a wax fire in the same way you would an oil fire. If your wax catches on fire, don't panic. Turn down the heat a bit, extinguish the fire, and get right back to dipping.

Before every season, I boil, dye, and wax all my traps to get them in perfect working order. I complete all the aforementioned tasks outdoors, and it only takes me a single Saturday to prepare all of my "seasoned" traps. I enjoy the time preparing my traps and snares just as much as scouting the areas where I plan on setting my trap line. Every trapper has his own routine for getting ready for the upcoming season. I cannot stress enough the importance of keeping everything scent free. I don't use any cover scents on my traps. Clean traps, without human scent, have always done well for me. Remember, you are in the animal's living room. Just like you can walk into your living room and notice instantly if something isn't quite right, wild animals will do the same. If you haven't taken the proper precautions, you greatly lessen your chances of trapping your food in a NONCON scenario.

ABOUT THE AUTHOR
STEPHEN KINNEY

Stephen grew up in the woods of North Carolina learning how to fish, hunt, trap and camp from family members. Practicing bushcraft and survival skills were what they called "playtime". He's always had a love for the outdoors and FOOD!! Stephen is an edged tool guy—meaning he likes working with knives, axes, saws, and pretty much all basic hand tools.

Stephen can be found on YouTube (Survival On The SKinney: https://bit.ly/2IzFtxu) and on INSTAGRAM (@skinney_survival). He can be reached at skinneyhunter@gmail.com. All photos in *Preparing Your Traps for the Field* by Stephen Kinney.

NONCON SKILL

HOW TO DRY AND PRESERVE MEAT

Drying meat is, by far, the best way to preserve it in the wild. Dehydrating meat removes the moisture that promotes bacterial growth. Dehydrated meat can be stored for months in a cool, dry place. The easiest method for dehydrating meat in a wilderness living situation is over the low heat of a small fire. The goal is to only DRY the meat, not COOK it. Cooking does not preserve it or make it last longer. You should be able to hold your bare hand underneath the meat drying rack. If the fire causes you to pull your hand away, it is too hot and the fire should be reduced in size. While it is possible to dry meat in the open air and full sun, the smoke from a fire keeps maggot-laying flies and other insects away. Smoke also imparts a good flavor to the dried meat. It is the dehydration, not the smoke, that preserves the meat.

Thinly sliced meat drying on a simple rack over a low fire.

Large leaved Burdock plant hung on top of the rack to protect from a slight rain drizzle during the drying period.

Drying meat does not cook the meat. It simply preserves it to last longer for cooking later. All dehydrated wild meats should be boiled or stewed before eating. Meat from large animals should be sliced into thin strips, no thicker than ¼-inch. Small game such as birds, rats, mice, or chipmunks can be dried whole and stewed in a Soup Sock (mentioned under the COOKING category of this manual) with other foods.

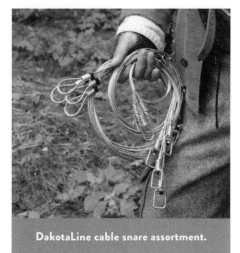

DakotaLine cable snare assortment.

Small game cable snare set across game trail (supported with Wire "N", detailed later).

Raccoon cuff trap.

QTY 9: Cable Snares: This is a kit purchased from DakotaLine Snares and it includes a total of 9 snares. Three different sizes of snares are included in this package. These various sizes allow you to catch animals from rabbits to wild hogs and everything in between. The small game snare is made from 3/64, 7x7 cable and is 30" long with an 11-gauge swivel on the anchor end. The medium game snare is made from 3/32, 7x7 cable and is 60" long with a 9-gauge swivel on the anchor end. The large game snare is made from 1/8, 7x7 cable and is 84" long with an adjustable loop on the anchor end. For many living in the south, where wild hogs are becoming more prevalent, the large game snare is an excellent snare to use on hog runs. Although I've never tried it, I'm convinced the large game snare could also catch a deer (ONLY in a survival scenario) if hung at head height along a deer path. Snare Lingo: 7x7 cable indicates that the cable has 7 cable wires, each made from 7 smaller wires. Another popular snare cable is 7x19 cable, which means there are 7 cable wires, each made from 19 smaller wires.

QTY 1: Raccoon Cuff Traps: I include this raccoon-specific trap because it is extremely easy to use and is highly effective. The brand I use is the Z-Trap Cross Fire, and the cost is about $20. These traps require the animal (typically a raccoon, although skunks and cats can get their paws in the hole too) to reach into the hole to grab the bait. When they do, the trigger fires and holds them tight. It's best baited with some old fish parts, and it can be placed in rock crevices, along embankments, or anywhere raccoons go.

NONCON SKILL

A PHOTO TUTORIAL FOR BUILDING
THE FIGURE-4 DEADFALL TRAP

If carved and set properly, I've found the Figure-4 Deadfall to be very effective on all small game animals up to roughly the size of a raccoon. The trigger system consists of three carved and notched sticks that hold together with tension provided by the deadfall weight. When the bait is disturbed, the sticks collapse under the weight of the deadfall and the quarry is crushed underneath. The photos below detail exactly how to make and set it (I have used colored sticks to help you with learning how to make and set this trap). Notice the "stick fence" I have placed around the trap. This is to force the animal through the front of the trap, which improves chances of capture.

Rat traps (one spray painted brown/green for camouflage).

QTY 3: Rat Trap: Chipmunks, rats, mice, and pine squirrel make perfect additions to wilderness stews and excellent bases for broth. There's usually not much left when cooked over a fire, but when boiled in water with some other wild edibles, they become quite a treat. These rat traps, when baited with locally harvested nuts or animal parts (tied onto the trigger pan), can put something in the pot almost every day. They are a wise addition to the survival trap line.

Be sure to place rat traps off the ground where predators can't readily find them. I prefer to set all rat traps (baited for rats, squirrel, and chipmunk) on poles leaning diagonally against trees. The traps should be fastened in place with 12-gauge wire (mentioned next) so they aren't taken or otherwise lost. See the sample set below for illustration.

Rat trap set on diagonal pole for squirrel (wire is twisted around trap to secure it to the pole).

Creek baiting squirrel pole rat trap with walnut.

12-Gauge Steel Galvanized Wire used to secure snare to tree.

50 Foot Coil 12-Gauge Steel Galvanized Wire: Wire has many uses, but this is packed specifically for use on the trap line. Heavy gauge wire serves many purposes. The three most frequent uses are for extending the reach of traps or snares from immovable objects, securing traps and snares to immovable objects, and positioning snare loops so they hang exactly where you want them.

NONCON SKILL

HOW TO SUSPEND A SNARE LOOP WITH THE WIRE "N"

Heavy gauge wire is the perfect solution for suspending and positioning snare loops across a trail or in front of a den hole. My method of choice is the wire "N". I have taken a photo that illustrates exactly how to do this.

If a tree or post isn't available on which to affix your heavy gauge wire "N", a wire support can be made (detailed in the two photos below). The upside-down "U" at the bottom prevents the wire support from rotating (as shown in the photo) when it is pressed into the ground.

Wire "N" for positioning snare noose.

Close-up of Wire "N".

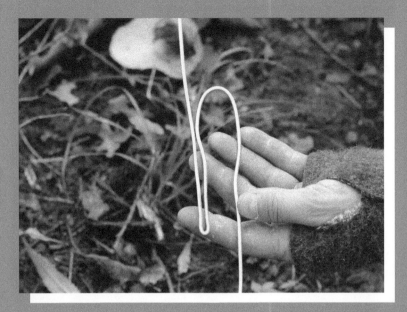

Upside down "U" at base of wire stake to prevent wire from rotating while in the ground.

Close-up photo of upside down "U" in ground.

CHAPTER

12

COOKING

With all kit items listed in the **FORAGING, FISHING, HUNTING,** and **TRAPPING** categories, you'd think I'd have more cooking implements included in my **NONCON** pack than I do. However, I keep it simple in the cooking department. I imagine cooking many meals over an open fire, using the pots and utensils listed below. For times when I don't have an open fire for cooking, my Kelly Kettle stove is an incredible little cooker that takes virtually no fuel (sticks and twigs) to operate. The details below cover my cooking and food prep items.

Kelly Kettle Stainless Scout Stove Kit (This kit includes the following items):

- **Large Stainless Steel Scout Kelly Kettle—41 oz.**

- **Large Stainless Steel Cookset—which includes 32 oz. pot, lid/frying pan, grill set, and pot gripper**

- **Large Stainless Steel Kelly Kettle Hobo Stove**

- **Two Stainless Steel Packable Kelly Kettle Cups with CooLip™ protectors and measurements inside (oz. and ml.)**

- **Two Packable Stainless Steel Plates/Bowls and Kelly Kettle carrying bag**

Kelly Kettle Stainless Scout Stove Kit.

Kelly Kettle in action (notice the very small fuel pieces it requires to operate).

Creek grilling frog legs on
Kelly Kettle grill top.

Grilling squirrel using
12"x12" grill over small fire.

Solo Stove Stainless Steel 1800 Pot.

Flexible plastic cutting board
(an invaluable food prep tool).

I can prepare almost any meal imaginable using this cook system, and I have on many occasions. In fact, I purchased a second one just for my NONCON Pack because I use my other one so often. I even cook meals on it at home when I'm out of propane for the grill and don't feel like running to the hardware store to get a refill. Between the pot, the grill, and the frying pan, it's a very flexible cook system. The only downfall is that the grill is a little small. Because of this, and because I do like the grilling option, I also pack a compact grill top that is about 12" x 12". This is a grill that I had custom made for APOCABOX subscribers. **If you desire one, they are available at http://www.creekstewart.com.**

12" x 12" Metal Grill Top (with handles): This small grill top (mentioned above) can be used for meats, plant stalks, and fish. It's small, lightweight, and durable. It can easily be set over a stone base or two green logs. This one comes with two small handles that make maneuvering over a fire or coals very easy.

Solo Stove Stainless Steel 1800 Pot: This is simply a second stainless pot with a holding capacity of 61 ounces. It has a lid, folding handles, and a bail for hanging over a fire. There are few things harder to manufacture in the wild than a cooking container. A pot-luck stew is my go-to wilderness hunter/gather meal. Fill the pot half full of water, throw in what meat items you have, along with wild greens, roots, and veggies and you will always have a warm and nutritious meal.

Flexible Plastic Cutting Boards (QTY 2): One food prep frustration I always have in the wild is the lack of a clean area to mix breads, cut up meat chunks, and prepare roots/greens for cooking or drying. I've solved this problem with two flexible cutting boards (from the Dollar Store) that slide along the back side of my pack and take up no space at all. They are very durable and extremely easy to clean. I keep two of these in all my food kits, and they work great in the field.

MAM Sheepsfoot Pocket Knife & Diamond Sharpener: This knife is dedicated for food prep only. It's a great little folder that is extremely sharp. I pair it with a small pocket diamond sharpener that ideally won't be used to sharpen other tools. Because I use my main survival knife (detailed later) for so many tasks, I prefer a dedicated knife for the final stages of food prep. **This MAM folder is perfect for that specific purpose, and it is available at http://www.creekstewart.com for $10 if you want one.**

Creek sharpening MAM Sheepsfoot knife with Diamond Pocket Sharpener.

Utensils: The only utensils I've packed are a small folding stainless spork and a folding MSR Alpine Spatula. I've found a spatula to be very helpful when using the frying pan. Of course, a suitable spatula can quickly be carved from a variety of woods as well.

MSR Alpine Spatula.

Pot/Utensil Scrubber: The cleaning scrubber I've been the happiest with, in terms of longevity, is the Coghlan's Stainless Steel Pot Scrubber, which costs around $5. If taken care of, this thing will last forever, and it cleans off dirt and cooking grime with ease.

Creek at stream edge cleaning soot from Kelly Kettle using Coghlan's Pot Scrubber.

Soup Socks (QTY 2): Soups socks are cotton mesh sacks designed for making flavorful and nutrient-rich, meat or vegetable broths, which are the perfect base for any wild soup or stew. I especially like using soup socks when cooking small game with lots of bones, like birds. You can fill a soup sock with birds that have been gutted and cleaned, then let them simmer in a pot of water filled with wild edible plants and tubers to make a magnificent broth. The birds can then be removed from the soup sock and eaten individually, without having fallen apart in the stew. Soup socks are also great for making broth from scrap meat parts, bones, random plant parts, and anything else you can think of. It's a great way to get the most use of your food items, keep the mess under control, and save yourself a lot of time.

Salt/Pepper Shaker preloaded with precious NOT-NONCON salt and pepper.

Salt/Pepper Shaker: Everything (and I mean EVERYTHING) tastes better when seasoned with salt and pepper. I have this little shaker pre-loaded with salt and pepper. Obviously, this is a consumable, however, I am familiar with many plants in the wild that can be used to make a variety of seasonings once the salt and pepper are gone. For example, the tiny black seeds from Garlic Mustard make an excellent horseradish-like seasoning. The whole seeds from Peppergrass and a variety of other mustard-like plants can be stored in this container and used as a pepper substitute.

NONCON SKILL

HOW TO IDENTIFY PEPPERGRASS

There are several varieties of Peppergrass, including Poor Man's Pepper, Cow-Cress, and Shepherd's Purse. They all look similar, and all the seeds have a peppery flavor. Poor Man's Pepper, often just called Peppergrass, is shown in the photos here. Notice the distinctive bottle-brush-like stalk of seed pods. This is the distinctive feature of Peppergrasses. The leaves of Peppergrass are toothed and stalked. There is one seed in each half of the slightly notched seed pod. In late summer, after the seed pods have dried, they can be collected in a pan and the outer sheaths are easily winnowed away in the wind, leaving the peppery seeds behind. The seeds are perfect for spicing up stews and meats when traditional pepper is not available. This plant is commonly found in disturbed areas, like construction sites and roadsides.

Peppergrass plant, notice bottle-brush-like features.

Toothed and stalked leaf of Peppergrass.

Seed pod containing pepper-flavored seeds.

Small pocket-sized can opener.

Can Opener: This little guy is reserved for the rare moments when I may need to open scavenged canned goods.

Strainer: Although I do not pack a strainer, there are a variety of items in my kit than can be used as one. These include a section of my screen drying rack (mentioned earlier), the MSR Alpine Spatula, and the pot with lid from my Kelly Kettle or Solo Stove Pot.

Small Game Gambrel: A gambrel is basically an upside-down, Y-shaped tool on which small game is hung during skinning and processing. It's an invaluable tool when routinely processing wild game. I've used the one shown to help skin every-thing from squirrel to raccoon.

Using gambrel to skin Red Fox Squirrel.

Heavy Duty Rubber Gloves: I've packed a pair of these primarily for cleaning and processing wild game. Although I've never been one to worry that much about using my bare hands to process wild game, I've also had the luxury of returning to modern civilization and its hygienic amenities after doing so. Without access to a modern medical facility (or even soapy water), I'm choosing to be safe and cautious. I will be using gloves in the field when processing wild meats. These are regular kitchen cleaning gloves that are available at any grocery store.

Creek skinning wild game using thick rubber gloves.

CHAPTER 16

TOOLS

Another heavy category is tools. There's just no way to shave much weight here. I've refined my tool selection over the last 20 years, and I have settled on the following assortment of tools to include in my NONCON pack. Hopefully, you will find something here that can add value to your own set of tools.

Creek's CS Slayback available at http://www.creekstewart.com.

Survival Knife: The knife I carry (at the time of this writing) is my own. It's called the CS Slayback and it is hand-forged from carbon steel in Kentucky. It's a great all-around carbon steel camp knife that is incredibly easy to maintain in the field. I carry a diamond rod and a bench stone for sharpening. The bench stone is a NORTON Pick-a-Pike Sharpening Stone and the size is 1"x 2"x 6". I used to watch my grandfather sharpen pocket knives to a razor's edge on this stone. I started using one after he passed away and use it still today. I put a new one in my NONCON Pack. Other survival knives I would highly recommend include any of the Whiskey Knives (http://www.whiskeyknives.com), the Blackbird SK5, and Morakniv Garberg. Each are high-quality, full-tang blades.

Chopping kindling with the Wetterlings Backcountry Axe.

Wetterlings Backcountry Axe: I use this axe for splitting kindling and light duty chopping to make campcraft items, such as furniture and cook systems. I also use it for driving trap stakes. Basically, the axe saves wear and tear on my knife. I use the Bahco Bow Saw (mentioned next) exclusively for large-scale wood processing.

Creek laying waste to a deadfall tree with the 30" Bahco.

Small folding saws are perfect for shelter building.

Cutting trapping wire using Leatherman MUT multi-tool.

Digging edible tuber with 18" pry bar.

Bahco 30" Bow Saw: This is one of the best tools I have ever purchased. I can process an incredible amount of firewood or shelter poles with it. It is a wood-sawing machine and easily cuts through 10" diameter logs. I would never go into the woods in cold weather for an extended period without this saw. I also carry two extra blades for it, which weigh almost nothing.

Folding Hand Saw: I also pack a folding hand saw with two extra blades. The Bahco Laplander and many different Silky saws are perfectly suited for a NONCON pack as well. I like the option to change out blades if necessary, so consider this when choosing one. Small folding saws are more portable for setting a trapline and day hikes, but they can also be work horses around camp for shelter building and campcraft.

Leatherman MUT Multi-tool: Any Leatherman Multi-tool will work fine; I just happen to like the MUT. It's important to make sure your multi-tool has pliers, wire cutters, a phillips head screwdriver, and a flat head screwdriver. I will use the wire cutters and pliers on this tool extensively while working with the heavy gauge wire that was detailed in the TRAPPING category.

18" Pry Bar: I've found pry bars to be very useful tools. They don't weigh or cost that much, so I've included one just in case I ever need it. This is a tool that saves wear and tear on other, more important tools. They also make an outstanding digging tool for latrine trenching and foraging. In fact, this pry bar serves as my backup digging tool for things like wild tubers and spruce root cordage if something happens to my foraging knife.

Sharpening Tools: As mentioned earlier, I carry two diamond sharpeners (one is dedicated solely to my food prep knife) and a 1"x 2"x 6" bench stone. I also carry a three-piece metal file set (round, half-round, and flat) for metal sharpening (including my Bahco Saw), steel trap maintenance, and wood-working (quick and easy notches for small game deadfalls).

Touching up 30" saw blade with small metal files.

Tool maintenance kit with needles, thread (2 kinds), and Speedy Stitcher Awl.

Aboriginal Woodshop Toolshop.

Goal Zero Guide 10 charging batteries.

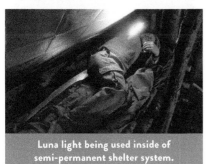
Luna light being used inside of semi-permanent shelter system.

Repair Tools: I carry an assortment of repair tools for sewing fabric or punching holes. The first of these is a Deluxe Speedy Stitcher Kit that includes the Speedy Stitcher Sewing Awl, a bobbin wound with 14 yards of waxed coarse thread, 4 needles (2 straight and 2 curved), and a 180-yard spool of additional waxed coarse thread. In addition to this kit, I have packed several repair needles for heavy gauge fabrics and a few spools of different threads, including a spool of Kevlar thread. I keep these needles in a small plastic test tube for protection, and I keep all the repair tools in a zipper canvas pouch. There is also a heavy-duty metal awl (such an important and underappreciated tool) in the Aboriginal Woodshop Toolshop Kit (detailed below).

Aboriginal Woodshop Toolshop: This is a small, portable kit of wood-working tools (manufactured for me by Reptile Toolworks in KY) that are worth their weight in gold for small projects, such as trap building, carving wooden utensils, basketry, and other wood-related campcraft endeavors. The kit includes a spoon knife, a chisel, a bow-sen, an awl, and two wooden handles. They all roll up into a small roll about 2" in diameter by 4" in length. If interested, these are available at http://www.creekstewart.com.

Goal Zero Guide 10 Battery Charger: This system is used to charge the batteries which power a few of the items listed next. This system directly charges a smartphone (though in a NONCON scenario, I doubt there will be cellular service available) in 1 hour of direct sunlight. It charges AA/AAA batteries and has a built-in LED light that runs for 150+ hours per charge. It came with 4 AA rechargeable batteries, and I have added in 6 more AA and 4 AAA as well. This kit has the Nomad solar panel and the power pack, which charges the batteries and connects via USB.

Luna LED Flexible Light Stick: This 1-watt LED stick light has 10 bulbs and is a perfect lightweight camp light. It's rated for 20,000 hours of use and can be powered from Goal Zero power packs or any USB port. It is 9 inches long and the snake-like cord is bendable, letting you secure it on shelter rafters or branches.

NONCON SKILL

HOW TO HAND SEW A LOCK STITCH WITH AN AWL

The Lock Stitch is a must-know sewing skill if you're ever going to make repairs in the field. This is the same stitch that a mechanical sewing machine makes, and it gets its name from the fact that the upper and lower threads lock together. Below is a photo tutorial of how to sew the Lock Stitch by hand.

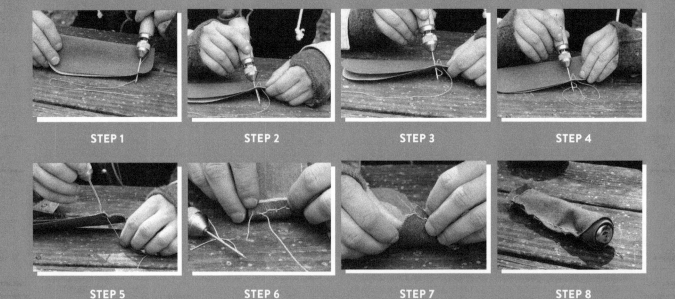

STEP 1   STEP 2   STEP 3   STEP 4

STEP 5   STEP 6   STEP 7   STEP 8

Petzl TIKKA Headlamp: This great little headlamp is powered by AAA batteries, which I can recharge with the Goal Zero Kit.

LuminAID Inflatable Lantern: This is a standalone solar-powered light that inflates to make a great camp lantern but breaks down small for transporting. Once fully charged, it has a max output of around 30 hours. It does take all day to fully charge. The product specs say it's good for up to 10,000 hours. I prefer the soft light of this lantern at night over the headlamp or the light stick.

Petzl TIKKA Headlamp.

Cobra RoadTRIP 40 Channel CB Radio: I figure CB Radio will be the primary mode of local communication if cell service drops. This portable radio is my best bet at staying in touch and listening in on local conversations. It runs on 9 AA batteries. It's a little bulky, but it's not very heavy.

LuminAID lantern solar light.

Listening to local chatter on CB Radio.

CHAPTER 14

FIRST AID & HYGIENE

Cotton cravat used for arm sling.

Two cotton cravats used as leg splint ties with SAM splint.

C.A.T. Tourniquet.

I have a friend who is an Army Special Forces Medic and has more Wilderness First Aid certifications than I could ever hope to amass in my lifetime. I asked him what to pack for first aid tools, keeping in mind that nothing could be consumable and that any injuries would likely take place in the field, without access to medical attention. He responded with the following four items:

Cravat 100% Cotton Triangular Bandages (QTY 4): These are sized 40 x 40 inches and are perfect for a multitude of first aid injuries. From bandaging and slinging sprained or broken arms to tying on sticks for splints, they are truly a multi-functional item.

SAM Splint: The SAM Splint is extremely moldable, and it is soft enough to cut with ordinary household scissors. It can be used to splint every bone in the human body and measures 36 x 4.25 inches.

C.A.T. Tourniquet: C.A.T. stands for Combat Application Tourniquet, and it is one of the fastest deploying tourniquets available on the market today. When a tourniquet is needed, nothing else will quite do the trick.

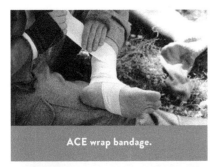
ACE wrap bandage.

ACE Wrap (3-Pack): For heavy bleeding, an elastic bandage, such as an ACE Wrap, can be a huge help. Once gauze (or a folded cravat bandage) is placed on the wound, it can then be wrapped with pressure using an elastic bandage. This helps to constrict the surrounding blood vessels and control severe bleeding while the body starts its natural clotting process.

Beyond these four pieces, I've also added the following items to my First Aid and Hygiene Category:

Creek's Blister Prevention & Treatment Kit (waterproof bag, leukotape, gauze pads).

Blister Treatment and Prevention Kit: Dealing with blisters (or preventing them) will probably be a routine occurrence in a NONCON scenario. This is a very simple blister kit that I have developed after trying every blister prevention and treatment method I have ever heard. It consists of a German made product called Leukotape and an assortment of gauze squares. Leukotape (available on Amazon) is a product designed for the athletic industry, and its adhesive is specifically designed to stick to skin—very active, wet, and sweaty skin. It is amazing stuff and will not come off until you pull it off. I have had Leukotape on my foot for a couple weeks at a time with no issues. Band-Aids, moleskin, and duct tape tend to fail soon after application, especially if they get wet. For preventing blisters, apply a layer of Leukotape to the skin where hot-spots are developing, before a blister forms. The boot or sock will rub against the tape instead of your skin, and it will prevent a blister from forming. For treatment, place a square of gauze over the blister and then place a piece of Leukotape across the gauze to allow the blister to heal. The gauze prevents the tape from sticking to the blister and ripping off the outer layer of skin when the tape is removed. The gauze pads are cut to size using the medical shears listed later in this chapter.

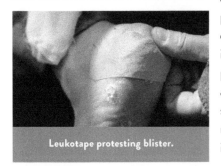
Leukotape protesting blister.

Large Packtowel: This is a towel that is 16.5" x 36" in size. It can soak up ten times its weight in water and wrings out almost completely dry. A towel is an underappreciated modern convenience and goes a long way for comfort in a wilderness living scenario.

Large Packtowel hanging from branch to dry.

6-piece tin assortment with samples of what they could be used for (melted beeswax, tallow, garlic mustard seeds, yarrow salve).

6-Piece Tin Assortment: This assortment includes a variety of both pressure fitted and screw top tins. They can be used to store any number of collected or processed items, including tallow (rendered fat), spices, medicinal plants, salves, etc.

Personal Mirror: Ever since I sustained an eye injury while hiking many years ago, I've never gone into the woods without a small, personal mirror. From tick checks to dealing with eye and facial issues, a mirror is a great kit piece. I use a mechanic's mirror with a small, expandable handle (which gives more flexibility) when trying to see hard-to-reach areas. It can also be used to see around corners.

Creek peering around corner with small Mechanic's Mirror.

Toothbrush: While a toothbrush might not last forever, and it is not technically NONCON, I'll put off using sticks and twigs to brush my teeth for as long as possible.

Bread Bag Clips (QTY 8)**:** These are the lightest and most effective clothes pins in the world.

Wound Irrigation Kit: Although this kit includes a couple of consumables, the main tool of interest is the irrigation syringe. Irrigating wounds to flush out bacteria and debris is essential for keeping infection at bay. The syringe can be boiled for sterilization and boiled water can be used for irrigating (boiled water, not BOILING water). This kit includes a 12cc Irrigation Syringe, ½ oz. betadine solution (antiseptic) and 4 individual 4"x4" non-sterile gauze pads contained in a zip-top bag.

Shirt hanging to dry on improvised clothesline (made utilizing the Timber Hitch and Trucker's Hitch) using two bread tie clips.

N-95 Debris Masks (QTY 3)**:** Inhaling toxic ash and debris from a burning city or forest can give you serious lung issues. Many are discovering this after surviving the tragedy of 9/11 in New York City. These simple, lightweight, and inexpensive masks are all one needs to prevent a gamut of long-term respiratory issues.

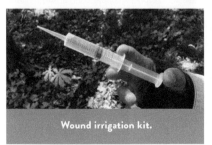

Wound irrigation kit.

N-95 Debris Mask.

NONCON SKILL

USING THE YUCCA PLANT AS SOAP FOR GEAR CLEANING AND HYGIENE

Although native to the American Southwest, species of Yucca can be found all over the United States. They can even survive through cold, harsh winters. Both the Yucca leaves and roots contain a chemical compound called Saponin, which produces a soap-like lather when vigorously mixed with water. This lather can be used to wash the body, hair, and gear, such as pots and pans. No special preparation is required. Simply crush the leaves or chunks of the peeled Yucca root and rub vigorously to activate Saponins, which will appear as a thin, white-green lather. As an interesting side note regarding ethnobotany (the study of the relationship between plants and humans), Saponins were also used by primitive cultures as a fish poison. Saponin-rich plants, such as the Yucca, were pulverized into a foamy paste and added to freshwater creeks and streams to stun and/or kill fish for easy collection.

Yucca plant that can be used for a primitive soap.

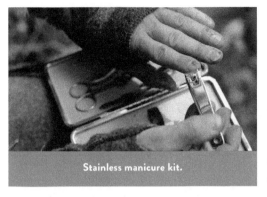
Stainless manicure kit.

Stainless Manicure Kit: Ignore the word "manicure". This 12-piece kit includes the following items: nail clippers, 2 pair of small scissors, nail file, slant edge clippers, toe nail clippers, tweezers, nail cleaner, cuticle cutter, cuticle pusher, cuticle trimmer, and ear pick. Although these tools aren't necessary, they certainly make personal hygiene a whole lot easier. Ask anyone who has had a bad ingrown toenail how it affects their ability to hike, and they'll tell you this kit would be a godsend. Keeping on top of hygiene helps to ward off infection, disease, and other illness. Hygiene is a very understudied and misunderstood survival category. Good hygiene is vital for long-term survival, especially in the woods.

Creek referencing Peterson Field Guide to Medicinal Plants and Herbs of Central and Eastern North America while studying wild medicinal plants (in this case, Goldenrod).

Peterson Field Guide to Medicinal Plants and Herbs of Central and Eastern North America: Medicinal herbs and plants tend to be one of my weakest subjects as a student of survival. While I certainly possess some knowledge on the subject, I have spent my career studying the ethno-botanical relationship between plants and humans on the levels of tools and food, not necessarily medicine. I have a vast knowledge of wild edible plants and how to use plants and trees for items such as baskets, cordage, and tools, but my skills are less impressive when it comes to sourcing medicines from the wild. For me, and others like me, a good field guide on medicinal plants is a critical addition to this category.

First aid shears being used to cut gauze squares in Creek's Blister Kit.

First Aid Shears: In addition to the small personal care scissors in my manicure kit, I've also packed these trauma shears. Though technically designed to cut through clothing, they are fantastic all-around shears for cutting fabrics, webbing, buckskin, fur-on hides, processed leather, natural fibers, and even thin bark.

NONCON SKILL

MEDICINAL YARROW

While Yarrow (*Achillea millefolium*) has many medicinal properties, one of the most unique is its ability to be used as a styptic. A styptic is a substance that helps to stop bleeding when applied to a wound. Yarrow has a rich history in times of war as a treatment for stopping blood flow. In fact, a couple of the common names for Yarrow are Soldier's Woundwort and the Nosebleed Plant.

According to the United States Department of Agriculture, Yarrow is prevalent in all 50 states, and I have personally seen it growing in Texas, California, Michigan, Kentucky, Tennessee, Florida, Georgia, North Carolina, and Indiana.

Yarrow rarely grows over 3 feet tall, which is one of the most prominent differentiating factors between it and a different (deadly) lacy white-flowered plant, called Poison Hemlock. Yarrow leaves literally look like green feathers. They are deeply dissected and pleasantly aromatic when crushed. They grow alternately along the stem.

The white Yarrow flowers grow in clusters on top of the plant. Each cluster consists of many tiny white flowers, as can be seen in the photo. Yarrow blooms from approximately May–July, depending on the area.

To use Yarrow as a styptic, it should first be dried, although it's not necessary. To do so, remove the leaves from the plant and place them in a cool, dry place. Because of the feathery nature, they'll be dry in just a couple of days.

To use them, simply crush the dried leaves and apply the powder to the wound. Not only will it help stanch the bleeding, but Yarrow also happens to have anti-inflammatory and anti-microbial properties too. All of these medicinal characteristics make Yarrow an outstanding wild plant to know.

CONCL

There is no doubt that **knowledge** concerning how to use NONCON gear is just as important as the gear itself. Conceptually, especially with a NONCON Pack, it is only the knowledge of how to use the gear that facilitates the acquisition of consumable survival resources, such as water, food, fuel, medicines, shelter, and fire. Even if one concludes that building a NONCON pack is beyond the scope of their own preparedness strategy, the previously mentioned collection of tools serves just as much purpose when stowed at home as it does inside of a backpack meant for the woods.

I will wrap up this manual with a word of encouragement and perspective. I am constantly contacted by individuals who feel overwhelmed by the process of preparing for disasters. Here is something that helps me: imagine there is a rope that goes on forever. Now imagine there is a piece of black tape wrapped around the first inch of that rope that goes on forever, as shown in the photo. As a survival instructor (and student of survival), it is very easy to get overwhelmed with having all the right skills and gear to survive what may or may not happen. To the person that feels this way, like I sometimes do, it's all about perspective. That one-inch section of black tape on that rope that goes on forever represents our life on Earth. The rest of that rope is our life after. It's OK if you're not prepared for everything that takes place on the inch of black tape-covered rope, because it's only a single inch on a rope that goes on forever. It's the rest of the rope that truly matters.

As always, I hope you've found something from this manual that you can implement into your own efforts and plans.

I hope you'll consider training with me at http://www.survivalskillofthemonth.com and http://www.wildedibleplantofthemonth.com.

Remember, it's not IF but WHEN,

CREEK
STEWART'S

THE ART
OF FIRE

MASTER THE ART OF FIRE IN CREEK'S MOST EXTENSIVE FIRE TRAINING SERIES YET!

ENROLL NOW AT
CREEKSTEWART.COM/ARTOFFIRE

NEVER WORRY ABOUT EATING A POISONOUS PLANT!

LEARN HOW TO IDENTIFY, HARVEST, AND EAT A NEW WILD EDIBLE PLANT EVERY MONTH!

DOWNLOAD A FREE WILD EDIBLE PLANT GUIDE NOW AT:
HTTP://WWW.WILDEDIBLEPLANTOFTHEMONTH.COM

SURVIVAL SKILL

OF THE MONTH CLUB

KNOWLEDGE
WEIGHS
NOTHING!

**MASTER A NEW SURVIVAL SKILL EVERY MONTH AND
JOIN A COMMUNITY OF SURVIVAL ENTHUSIASTS!**

SURVIVALSKILLOFTHEMONTH.COM

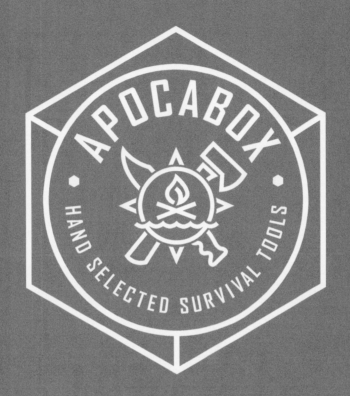

APOCABOX

HAND SELECTED SURVIVAL TOOLS

MYAPOCABOX.COM

IT'S LIKE SURVIVAL CHRISTMAS EVERY OTHER MONTH!